TUNISIA

By the staff of Editions Berlitz

Berlitz Trademark Reg. U.S. Patent Office
and other countries – Marca Registrada.
Library of Congress Catalog Card No. 79-84586.

Printed in Switzerland by Weber S.A., Bienne.

Updated edition 1982

Preface

A new kind of travel guide for the jet age—and one of an extensive series by Berlitz on the world's top tourist areas—this compact and colourful book is packed with all you need to know about Tunisia.

Like our phrase books and dictionaries, this book fits your pocket—in both size and price. It also aims to fit your travel needs:

- It combines easy reading with fast facts: what to see and do, where to shop, what to eat.

- An authoritative A-to-Z "blueprint" fills the back of the book, giving clear-cut answers to all your questions, from "Where can I change traveller's cheques after normal banking hours?" to "Is the water safe to drink?" plus how to get there, when to go and what to budget.

- Easy-to-read maps in full colour pinpoint sights you'll want to see.

In short, this handy guide will enhance your enjoyment of Tunisia. From the ancient Roman ruins of Carthage to the *souks* of modern Tunis, from the luxurious beach resorts of Cap Bon and Djerba to the burning deserts of the Tunisian South—Berlitz tells you clearly and concisely what it's all about.

Let your travel agent help you choose a hotel.

Let a restaurant guide help you find a good place to eat.

But to decide "What should we do today?", travel with Berlitz.

Area specialist: Tom Brosnahan
Photography: Claude Huber
Layout: Aude Aquoise
We are particularly grateful to William Graham and Mary Nicholson for their help in the preparation of this book. We also wish to thank the Office National du Tourisme Tunisien for their valuable assistance.

4 *Falk* Cartography: Falk-Verlag, Hamburg.

Contents

Tunisia and the Tunisians 6

A Brief History 10

Where to Go

    Tunis 24

    Cap Bon Region 38

    The Sahel 42

    Djerba 51

    Southern Tunisia and the Desert 60

    The Far North 75

What to Do

    Sports 79

    Folklore 82

    Festivals 84

    Shopping 86

    Nightlife 90

Wining and Dining 92

How to Get There and When to Go 100

Planning Your Budget 103

Blueprint for a Perfect Trip 104

Index 127

Maps: Tunis p. 25, Northern Tunisia p. 39, Southern Tunisia p. 61.
Picture (pages 2–3): Desert near Kébili. *Cover:* "Barber's Mosque", Kairouan.

How to use this guide
If time is short, look for items to visit which are printed in bold
type in this book, e.g. **Cap Tourgueness.** Those sights most highly
recommended are not only given in bold type but also carry our
traveller symbol, e.g. **Matmata.**

Tunisia and the Tunisians

Never in its long and glittering history has Tunisia been more bountiful or accommodating than it is today. Every region of the country has some special beauty and allure. Cap Bon juts out into the eastern Mediterranean, a vast garden paradise of citrus groves and flower gardens bordered by a wide ribbon of warm sandy beach. Along the northern coast, fishermen's skiffs rock and bob in coves where pirates once lurked.

Typically Tunisian scenes: geometric cityscape of Sousse and (right) colourfully clad Djerban woman heading home from the well.

Now divers, professional and amateur alike, come up with twigs of bright, gem-like coral. In Hammamet and Nabeul, a medieval fortress shares the beach with luxury resort hotels. Palm groves provide shade, and thickets of jasmine, wisteria and bougainvillea add colour and fragrance. To the south in Sousse and Monastir, straw-hatted tourists jostle veiled Tunisian women in flowing robes along the narrow streets of the *médinas.* Even farther south, the Isle of Djerba is the legendary land of the Lotus-Eaters which tempted Ulysses and his crew.

The Greek heroes were not the only ones to be attracted by Tunisia's mild climate and rich landscape. The Phoenicians founded Carthage near what is now Tunis, and they built a vast Mediterranean empire around it. Then the Romans made the short hop across the straits of Sicily, conquered Carthage and established the

first Roman province on the southern continent. They called it Africa.

In Roman Africa at harvest-time, a thousand camels a day were loaded with grain for the larders of the capital; fish nets from hundreds of boats strained under the weight of the catch; oranges from coastal groves and dates from desert oases graced the Roman patrician's table, and wine from the vineyards filled his cup. In return, the conquerors nurtured the land, built cities and roads, aqueducts and temples. Today, Tunisia's museums preserve their art, which gloried in the bounty and beauty of the country: countless striking mosaics portray hunting scenes, the harvest of grape and grain, the dozens of game animals and marine delicacies which were enjoyed by the lords of Africa.

After the Romans came others: Teutonic Vandals from central Europe, Byzantines from Constantinople, Arabs and Turks, Normans from Scandinavia via Sicily, all mixing with the mysterious and ferociously independent people known as Berbers who had been there since prehistoric times.

The long 19th- to 20th-century French presence in Tunisia left the country a legacy of good roads and communications, hospitals, schools and public institutions. The French influence is visible in all aspects of Tunisian life and especially notable on restaurant menus. Once you've savoured the tempting local *couscous* and *tajine,* you can pamper your appetite with a good *chateaubriand.* Even if the waiter doesn't speak your language, he'll catch on quickly to a few words of French. And, should you attempt a word of thanks in Arabic, you'll have made a friend for the rest of your stay.

Tourists are the latest "invaders" of Tunisia, coming by air or car-ferry, heading for sunny beaches, pristine white villages and peaceful desert oases.

But, with the beaches so accessible, so numerous and so warm, it's all too easy to get a burn rather than a tan: the thing to do is to alternate sunning with sightseeing or sport. Play a few sets of tennis, or take an excursion on horseback. Sign up for a trip by Land-

Ancestors of caretaker in La Ghriba, Djerba's synagogue, fled Jerusalem some 2,500 years ago.

Rover to an oasis or to some Berber *ghorfas*, the fortified stone "beehives" where the nomads stored their valuables. Spend an hour touring a mighty *ribat*, a fortress-like monastery once inhabited by pious Moslem warriors, or hire a car and visit the coastal villages or desert towns. Even the most humble have a few lazy outdoor cafés where you can while away the time with a bottle of mineral water or a glass of sweet mint tea. Suitably refreshed, plunge into the *souks* draped with soft carpets and colourful *mergoums* (embroidered mats) and piled with gleaming copper, gilded leather, fragrant spices and quaint jewellery. You needn't worry about getting lost, for at the first sign of perplexity the nearest child will volunteer his services as a guide. He will certainly speak French, perhaps some English or German as well, and will tell you all about everything for just a few *bonbons* or *une pièce* (a coin).

Let the sun be your alarm clock in Tunisia, it's dependable 300 days a year. Let fascination be your guide, let the gracious and friendly Tunisians be your hosts and helpers. You're sure to return home with more than just a suntan and a new pair of sandals.

A Brief History

Tunisia is an ancient land. People first walked here as long ago as 6,000 B.C., leaving behind potsherds and rude tools which tell us of their culture. But the first men to settle permanently and to record their adventures in writing were the Phoenicians who founded Utica (12th century B.C.) and then Carthage (814 B.C.). These intrepid explorers and traders spread throughout the Mediterranean world from Tyre and Sidon on the Levant (Lebanese) coast, beginning in the 15th century B.C. Soon they became masters of the sea.

The Phoenicians were clever as well as brave, and to record their commercial dealings they adopted a clever alphabet based on sounds—to replace the cumbersome cuneiform writing. But despite advances these were brutal times, and over the centuries thousands of first-born sons and daughters, sheep and goats were sacrificed to the vengeful god of the Phoenicians, Baal Hammon. Hundreds of funerary stones describing the sacrifices have been uncovered in *tophets*, the sacred places near Phoenician cities where the bloody rites were held.

Dynastic rivalries in the home cities allowed Carthage to gain more and more power, and when Tyre and Sidon fell to Cyrus the Great of Persia (6th century B.C.), Carthage became undisputed queen of Punic (Phoenician) civilization. From North Africa to southern Spain, from the eastern Mediterranean to the Atlantic, Carthaginian settlements were established. Carthaginian captains commanded the straits of Sicily and fought the Greeks for rule of the seas.

Roman Africa

One of Carthage's neighbours at this time was a small kingdom centred on the town of Rome, founded in the 8th century B.C. Although for a long time the Romans had been preoccupied in extending and consolidating rule within their own peninsula, the threat posed by the extent of Carthaginian power in the Mediterranean was too great to be ignored, quite apart from the growing ambitions of the rising nation.

Lashed to ship's mast, Ulysses listens to Sirens' song; crew have ears stopped with wax, eyes averted from temptation (Bardo Museum).

Rome conquered Carthage in the three Punic Wars (3rd–2nd centuries B.C.), but not without some reverses. In a naval battle during the first Punic War, the Roman admiral Claudius Pulcher consulted the sacred chickens which were kept aboard his flagship, asking for an omen. The chickens were supposed to peck at their grain if he was to win, but seasickness or general lack of inclination did its work, and there wasn't a single peck from a single chicken. Claudius, a proven hothead, tossed the sacred chickens overboard to the applause of his crew and charged into battle. He lost his entire fleet.

Another major defeat for the Romans was during the second Punic War. Setting out from Spain, Hannibal, the Carthaginian general, crossed the Alps with more than 30,000 men and two or three dozen elephants. He clashed with the Roman army in 216 B.C. The battle, at Cannae in southern Italy, was a devastating blow for the Romans, who lost over 50,000 men.

But despite the setbacks, in the end the Punic lands became the Roman province of Africa in 146 B.C. Right after the conquest Carthage was destroyed. Then, in 44 B.C., Julius Caesar laid plans for its reconstruction. Within two centuries it was a city of almost 300,000. Other Roman cities, each with their triumphal arches, temples. forums and, later on, churches, were built up and flourished.

Tunisia remained Roman for about 600 years, but when the barbarian hordes swept through Europe in the 5th century, neither the Roman soldiers nor the Mediterranean sea could deter them. By A.D. 439, an army of Germanic tribesmen, the Vandals, had invaded the country led by one Genseric, who became lord of Carthage. The Vandal leader looked upon the land as his own personal property, and didn't take the steps necessary to set up a formal government. When he died, the country broke down in anarchy. It was easy for the Byzantine emperor Justinian to send an army to take over in 534. Succeeding emperors in Constantinople held onto Tunisia for slightly over a century, until the momentous Arab invasions.

Visitors to Sousse brave mosaic Medusa's curse: but even close up, she turns no one to stone.

The Arab Empire

No one knows exactly why a few dozen tribes of Semites living in hot and dusty Arabia should have begun to dream of world conquest, but so they did. Arab tribes had raided one another for centuries, but under the guidance of the Prophet Mohammed the tribes got together, settled their differences and formed the community of Islam (or, "submission to God's will").

It all started when Mohammed, a merchant, received the revelation of the Koran. He was a pensive sort who would go off to a cool cave in the mountains to think and ponder, and during one such retreat in the year 610 he heard the voice of God say, unmistakably, "Write!". What he produced was the most breathtakingly beautiful work ever to exist in Arabic. The Koran became the poetry, inspiration, and law code of the Arabic people. When Mohammed died (632), his followers elected a devout Moslem as caliph, or deputy, to rule in his place.

Armed with religious inspiration in addition to the sword, the Arab armies set out and within a century (634–732) had conquered, and partly converted, all the Middle East including Persia, all of North Africa and Spain, and part of France.

Of the early Arab warriors, none was bolder than Oqba Ibn Nafi, conqueror of the Maghreb.* With the blessing of the ruling caliph, Oqba conquered what he called Ifriqiya (Roman Africa). Ignoring the infidel city of Carthage, he established his own capital at Kairouan in 671, saying, "I shall build a town to be a citadel of Islam for all time". From there the impulsive swordsman of Islam set off to the west. When he got to the Atlantic Ocean, he called God to witness that he stopped only because he had run out of infidels to convert or conquer. The lands of the Maghreb were to remain Moslem until the present day.

But conquest, and then governing the conquered lands, was not as easy as it looked. The Arabic Empire, which had started out in a pure, simple, commune-like state in Arabia ruled by Mohammed, was now a tremendous, far-flung, complex entity. Dozens of different peoples living in the Arab dominions spoke scores of

---

* The names "Maghreb" and "Barbary" both refer to the region of North Africa between the Atlantic and Tunisia (or sometimes Libya), bounded by the Sahara in the south and the Mediterranean in the north.

Five Pillars of Islam

A Moslem has five important duties, and without observing these he cannot really be a good Moslem. First, he must show he has accepted Islam by saying, "There is only one God, and Mohammed is His Prophet". Second, he must perform a very carefully prescribed ritual of prayer five times a day—the muezzin gives a call to prayer at the proper hours so Moslems will know when. Third, a Moslem must observe the fast of Ramadan, which means no eating, drinking, smoking, or even licking a stamp during daylight hours. (Ramadan is a month of the lunar calendar, and so its exact dates change from year to year.) Fourth, Moslems must be charitable and give a certain portion of their goods to the community and to the poor. Fifth, if it is possible, each Moslem should make the pilgrimage *(hadj)* to the holy city of Mecca at least once in his life. Many other rules of moral and spiritual conduct are part of a good Moslem's life, but these five are the indispensible tenets, the "Five Pillars" which support the commonwealth of Islam.

languages and held tight to their ancient traditions, Moslem or not. The Berbers, inhabitants of the lands north of the Sahara for no one knows how long, were one example of a people who weren't inclined to follow Arab customs. Shortly after Oqba's invasion of Ifriqiya, a counter-thrust was made by a nomadic Berber tribe of the Jewish religion. They were led by a powerful queen known as "The Prophetess" *(Kahina)*. Much of the land was recaptured by her forces, and it took the Arabs five years before they were able to put down the revolt. The Kahina was executed and her head sent to the caliph in Damascus on a platter.

By this time the great city of Carthage was in ruins, so the Arabs started to build up Tunis nearby to be the northern stronghold of the country in 698.

In some ways the Arab conquest had little effect on Tunisia. Though Islam is the religion of most Tunisians, and Arabic the main language, the culture, traditions and even the people themselves remain a cosmopolitan mixture of wildly different elements. While the Arab armies swept through and took control, they were not followed by hordes of colonists and settlers, and Tunisians continued to be an assortment of peoples (Berber, Carthaginian, Roman, Vandal, Byzantine and now also Arab) who didn't take kindly to outside control.

From the 8th century onward, this spirit of independence affected even the governors sent by the conquering empire. The Aghlabid dynasty, which ruled Tunisia from 800 to 909, was begun by one Ibrahim ibn Aghlab. He had been sent by the caliph of Baghdad to be governor in Tunis, but he ended up an independent prince who ruled not only Tunisia but also Sicily, Malta, Sardinia and even parts of southern Italy. The Aghlabids put together a regular government, rebuilt the Grand Mosque at Kairouan and generally did much to bring stability to the country. But order on a large scale was the problem—nobody except the government really wanted it. Soon the Aghlabids were replaced by the Fatimids whose empire extended to Egypt. Then came a dynasty called the Zirids, who were later overcome by unruly nomadic Arabs of the Beni Hilal tribe. And so it continued, each group ruling Tunisia as best it could—for a time.

In the middle of the 12th century, a powerful family, the Almohads, based in the Moroccan city of Marrakesh, marched in from the west and ruled for 70 years, bringing prosperity, religious severity and orderly government. But again, the temptation to "go native" was too much for the governors, and they broke away from the Almohad empire to found their own dynasty, the Hafsids (1228–1574).

With Tunis as their capital the Hafsids grew in power and splendour. The two most famous religious schools *(médersas)* in Tunis and the picturesque *souks* of the perfumers *(Attarine)* and cloth-merchants *(Koumach)* are but a few of their architectural contributions. The great Abu Abdullah al-Mustansir (1249–77) took the title "Commander of the Faithful", which was as good as proclaiming himself caliph of all Moslems. In 1270, a crusade was undertaken against al-Mustansir, with France's heroic King Louis IX at the head of the army; but the crusade failed, and Louis died in Tunis.

Groups of Moslem pilgrims come from many countries to admire Kairouan's stately Grand Mosque

The mighty walls of Monastir's medieval ribat, *specially designed and built to repel invaders, now yield daily to scores of tourists.*

Turks and Pirates

Though the Hafsids had started out well, like all central governments in Tunisia they ended being hated by the freedom-loving Berber nomads. The officials' high-handed methods alienated city-dwellers as well. And so, when the swashbuckling Turkish corsair Haireddin Barbarossa (Redbeard) appeared on the scene in 1534, the people of Tunis welcomed him as a conquering hero. Nevertheless, the country remained in the hands of the Hafsids until 1574 when it became part of the Ottoman empire.

With the Turks' arrival

manoeuverable than sailing ships. Discipline and order were rigid at sea, and any man who moved from his station or was slack in his duties was summarily strangled. A pirate galliot would race up to a merchantman or a coastal town, attack, take prisoners and booty, and speed away almost before the unfortunate victims knew what had happened. When the pirates returned in triumph to Tunis, the whole town would explode with feasting and merry-making. Every man of the crew would be rich—even the galley-slaves who pulled the oars—after he sold his portion of loot. The merchants of Tunis bought all the swag and later disposed of it at a good profit. Christian prisoners were sold into slavery, and brought good prices if they were craftsmen or had other special skills. Any nobles or wealthy merchants who were captured were quickly ransomed—the slave dealers would examine their clothes and hands to see who might bring a good price.

Tunisian pirates in the 17th and 18th centuries made their country rich and powerful, and were soon operating independently of the Turkish sultan. The bey of Tunis, who had originally been appointed ev-

came might as a medieval sea power. The corsairs, particularly active in the Christian slave trade, became the terror of all shipping that was not Ottoman. Two infamous sea captains of this time were Dragut and Ali; they were followed by other pirate captains who attracted mercenaries and soldiers-of-fortune from all over the Mediterranean basin. Their ships, called galliots, were powered by oars and were faster, less easily visible, and more ery three years by the sultan, now started to pass on his position by heredity. In the late 1700s, the Turkish beys were so deeply absorbed into Tunisian culture that they were in fact Tunisians in everything but name.

Under Ahmed Bey (1837–55), the country made its first major attempt to jump from a medieval Islamic society into the modern world. Slavery was abolished and European aid was sought to build a modern army. New factories, banks and communications were set up. But Europe was too fast and too far ahead of the Moslem world. The pirate ships of the Barbary coast were outrun and driven from the seas by the swifter and mightier European ironclads powered by steam. Soon the once proud pirate states had become "protectorates", and their treasuries, armies and governments were under European control.

A Tunisian bey was on the throne all through the time that France ruled Tunisia (1881–1956), but he was a mere figurehead. The country was in a bad way and the reforms ordered by the French were meant to restore prosperity. Just how the balance-sheet of these years of French control can be drawn up is still a subject for endless arguments. How much did France as a whole, and the French settlers in particular, gain at the expense of Tunisia? What benefits were brought by the French in return? Whichever way you look at it, the Tunisians wanted to govern themselves.

Struggle for Independence

For almost a century Tunisians had had the opportunity to study European ways firsthand. Many spoke French as well as any Frenchman, and many had great abilities but were not allowed to use them. In short, the country was ready for independence.

The first liberation movement was launched in Tunis the very same year in which the French occupation began (1881). Later, in 1907, the "Young Tunisian Party" was founded. This small group mostly thought or wrote about revolution. But in 1911 a bloody uprising known as the Jellaz affair brought a lot more Tunisians of all social levels into the nationalist movement. Clearly, sympathy for independence was growing.

The First World War kept the new movement from any action, but right after the war, in 1920, the Liberal Constitutional Party, or Destour, was organized. The aim of the Destour Party was to work with the French towards more Tunisian autonomy, but the policy was to end in inertia and failure. A new shot of spirit was needed.

In 1927, a young Tunisian of exceptional ability arrived home, having just finished his education in Paris. Habib Bourguiba was filled with French thoughts and sentiments, and he sympathized with the Destour at first. But he soon concluded that there could be no progress without struggle, and forcefully expressed these views through newspaper articles. In 1934 he founded the Neo-Destour Party with a group of friends, and in that same year was arrested as a political agitator and sent to jail for three years.

With the onset of the Second World War, and especially after the defeat of France by Germany in 1940, Tunisia became involved in the struggle between the Allies and the Axis powers for control of the Mediterranean and North Africa. When the Allies under General Eisenhower landed in North Africa in November 1942, the Germans and Italians seized Tunisia as a vital base for the operation Rommel was carrying out farther east, towards the Suez Canal. The area became the scene of fierce fighting between the Germans and Commonwealth and American forces until finally the Allies triumphed in May 1943.

Meanwhile the Axis powers had sought in vain to win over Bourguiba to their side. But by 1945, the prospect of obtaining major concessions from France by negotiation did not seem good to him either, and he left Tunisia to set up a Committee for the Liberation of the Maghreb in Cairo. Travelling extensively and spreading the idea of independence, by 1948, Bourguiba had become a noted figure and president of the Destour Party. The French, recognizing that negotiations would have to be held with Bourguiba, invited him to Paris. Talks were held: Tunisia was to be autonomous. But the promises were not implemented and armed groups of patriots started to resort to more militant tactics. When Bourguiba returned to his country he was again arrested and thrown into jail.

Bourguiba's arrest inflamed already swollen passions, and bloody clashes became frequent. Among the French settlers in the country, there was fierce resistance to the idea of concessions on the part of **21**

Talking Tunisian

Listed below is a mini-vocabulary which you'll find useful during your stay in Tunisia:

aïn	spring
bab (pl. *bibane*)	entrance, gate
bordj	fort
chott	salt lake
dar	house
djamâ	mosque
(d)jebba/ (d)jellaba	long sleeved tunic
djébel	mountain
el	the
erg	region of sand dunes
ghorfa	fortified stone house
hadj	pilgrimage (to Mecca)
kalaâ	fortress
kasba	citadel; fortified part of *médina*
klim	woven carpet with geometric design
ksar	fortified village
maqroudh	semolina sweet-meats made with syrup and date paste
médersa	(religious) school
médina	old town
mergoum	embroidered mat/carpet
ribat	fortified monastery
souk(s)	market (streets)
tophet	place of sacrifice
zaouïa	house of a religious order
zerbia	knotted carpet

Paris; but in 1954 the French premier, Mendès-France, publicly recognized Tunisia's right to self-government, and in the following year a new French premier, Edgar Faure, met officially and publicly with Bourguiba to sign a protocol granting Tunisia its internal autonomy. Habib Bourguiba returned to Tunis in triumph. Within a year the country was fully independent (although France retained the military base of Bizerta until 1963).

In April 1956, the Tunisian leader was elected President of the Council (premier), but the country was still nominally ruled by the bey. With the deposition of the bey in 1957, Tunisia became a republic and Habib Bourguiba was elected its first president. So well did President Bourguiba embody the spirit of Tunisian independence that he was overwhelmingly re-elected to three more terms as president, and finally elected President-for-Life. The age-old dream of Tunisia for the Tunisians had been realized at last.

A smiling President Bourguiba is a suitable backdrop for this young Tunisian's musical efforts.

Where to Go

The chances are that you're heading to Tunisia to find the sun—on the beach, in a deck chair or out on the tennis courts. Lots of places along the coast offer possibilities for soaking in the healthful rays. From these sun spots, short trips to the interior of the country are an excellent diversion and also the best way ever to experience Tunisia and the Tunisians. In this section we cover the major travel possibilities—from lush, sybaritic resorts to the spare, elemental vastness of the desert—beginning with the Republic's busiest and most colourful city.

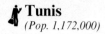

Tunis
(Pop. 1,172,000)

Tunis is actually three cities in one. First, there's the modern capital of the Tunisian Republic, a city of wide tree-lined boulevards, lofty buildings and bustling sidewalk cafés. Then, there's the medieval Arab *médina*, a mysterious and exciting maze of narrow, angled streets lined with tiny shops, grand mosques and impressive palaces; and finally there's Carthage, the ancient city 18 km. (12 miles) from the centre of modern Tunis, surrounded by flower-decked suburban villas. You can easily spend two full days exploring Tunis and surroundings, though a day-and-a-half will serve if you're short on time.

The lifeline of modern Tunis is **Avenue Habib Bourguiba,** stretching from the port on the Lake of Tunis to Place de l'Indépendance. A stroll along its shady central promenade gives most visitors their first taste of the city's life. Kiosks stacked with newspapers, magazines and books alternate with alluring flower stalls along the promenade. Several of the capital's luxury hotels are on the avenue, as well as a dozen outdoor cafés, large and small.

At the western end, Place de l'Indépendance is dominated by the cathedral of St. Vincent de Paul (1882). A symbol of former Catholic rule in a Moslem land, the cathedral beckons to would-be converts, and a high-relief figure on the façade has arms outstretched, coaxing passers-by to come in and have a look.

From the square, it is only a few blocks' walk along the Avenue de France to the *médina*, or old city.

TUNIS

LA SOUKRA

CARTHAGE LA MARSA

0.5 km
0.5 miles

Parc du Belvédère

Centre d'Art vivant

Parc zoologique

Place Pasteur

Av. Dr. Ch. Nicolle

Avenue Mohamed V

Avenue Kheireddine Pacha

Cimetière Municipal

Cim. Grec.

Cim. Israélite

LAFAYETTE

EL OMRANE

Av. Ouled Haffou

Av. Bechir Sfar

esne ben Chaâbane

Bd. Hédi Saïdi

Avenue Taïeb Mehiri

Av. Hédi Chaker

Av. Ch. Kallala

Av. de la liberté

Avenue Mohamed V

Lac de Tunis
(El Bahira)

N

Bab el Khadra

Av. de Lyon

Avenue de Madrid

Parc J. F. Kennedy

Av. du Ghana

Place de la République

Parc des Sports

BAB SOUIKA

Rue Bab Bou Saadoun

Av. Ali Belhaouane

R. Bab Souika

Av. de Londres

R Monci Slim

Parc H. Thameur

Av. H. Thameur

Avenue de Paris

CARTHAGE

Avenue du 9 Avril 1938

Bab Souika

Bd Bab Benat

Mosquée Sidi Mahrez

MEDINA

Mausolée Hammoûda Pacha

Porte de France

Cathédrale

Pl. de l'Indépendance

Av. de France

Gamal

Office National du Tourisme

Avenue Habib - Bourguiba

Pl. d'Afrique

Gare T.G.M.

R.P. Bourde

Bd Bab Benat

Kasbah

Dar el Bey

Mosquée Djamâ ez Zitouna

Poste

Av. de France

Av. Farhat Hached

Municipalité

Gare

Port

ASSINE

Dargbouth Pacha

M. Khaznadar

Mosquée de la Kasbah

Dar Hussein

Dar ben Abdallah

SOUKS

Av. Bab Menara

Rue Sidi el Bechir

Av. Monçef Bey

Rue de Turquie

Rue de la République

Av. de Carthage

Av. de Paris

Pt Khairoun

Av. Franklin

Gare des Marchandises

MONTFLEURY

Parc El Gorjani

Avenue du 9 Avril 1938

Bab Alleoua

Cimetière de Djellaz

Av. des Félibres

THUBURBO MAJUS, EL FAHS, KAIROUAN

SOUSSE

The Médina

The Porte de France (1848) marks the entrance to the *médina*, once surrounded by thick walls. To the right of the gate is the British embassy, in a picturesque Moorish building straight out of the *Arabian Nights*. Walk straight through the Porte de France and then slightly to the left to reach Rue Djamâ ez Zitouna, the *médina's* main street.

As you plunge into this strange and ancient town, all of your senses will be sharpened. Bright colours and muted shades, shiny copper and rusty iron, glittering jewellery and the soft patina of fine leather offer striking contrasts. Fragrant incenses and perfumes compete with the mouth-watering smell of roasting mutton and the aroma of freshly ground coffee. The clatter of craftsmen's hammers and the scuff of sandalled feet on the smooth paving stones almost drown the muezzin's call to prayer wafting from a minaret.

Centre-piece of the *médina* is the grand mosque, **Djamâ ez Zitouna** (Mosque of the Olive Tree). For over a thousand years it was the focus of daily life here. First built in 732, the mosque was enriched and expanded many times as the centuries passed, and was last re-novated less than 20 years ago. Only Moslems are allowed to enter to see the intricate tracery done in plaster, the crystal lamps and the forest of columns, marble and breccia. But from 8 to 11 a.m. every morning (except Fridays), any visitor is allowed to climb the stairs to the arcade for a look

around. Though it's unlikely that you'll get a glimpse of the interior from here, you can be certain a self-appointed "guide" will approach you, and for a few hundred Millimes will tell you as much or more than you want to know about the mosque.

The most interesting sections

Bits of tile add colour to a roof-top terrace in Tunis' médina.

of the bazaar are clustered near the grand mosque. In the course of the *médina's* thousand-year-old history, these narrow streets were covered with vaulted roofs to make cosy **27** quarters for the city's artisans and tradesmen. Members of high-class guilds like the perfumers, booksellers and jewellers got the best places, close to the mosque, whereas metalworkers and saddlers, who made a clatter when they worked, were located some distance away as otherwise this might disturb the recitation of the ninety-nine names of God. The unlucky tanners, necessary but noxious, were banished even farther afield to the other side of the city walls.

Tourism and new merchandising methods have wrought havoc with this neat department-store layout of the bazaar. Though several of the old *souks* (market streets) are still predominantly inhabited by masters of one traditional guild, it's more usual to see a variety of different shops in a single *souk*.

Don't miss the **Souk el Attarine,** along the north wall of the Zitouna mosque. Each little shop is stacked with hundreds of tiny bottles holding priceless essences: rose oil, almond oil, oils of lemon and clove. You can choose a scent already mixed, or have one blended to suit your whim or fancy. By the way, the curious, many-branched candles hanging in the perfumers' shops are used after the perfume has done its work: they are carried at the head of the procession which takes a bride to her new home.

Along the west wall of the Zitouna is one of the quietest *souks,* the **Souk el Koumach** (drapers). Hanging cloths and blankets muffle the spirited haggling of the shopkeepers. A short distance from the southwest corner of the mosque is the **Souk des Orfèvres,** a warren of tiny streets and alleys crowded with gold and silversmiths' shops. The ring of small hammers and the hiss of forges come from a dozen doorways, and shop-windows glitter and shine with gold, coral, pearls and precious stones.

Denizens of the *médina,* those who stroll its streets daily, know its secrets: behind this battered wooden door, a cosy family *qbou* (parlour), behind that massive portal studded with iron, a sumptuous palace. The palaces, in fact, are the buildings most easily accessible to tourists. Many of them are museums or public buildings. **Dar Hussein,** a palace of the 18th century, south of the

Tunis shop windows ablaze with gold, silver and precious stones: tempting presents for all the family.

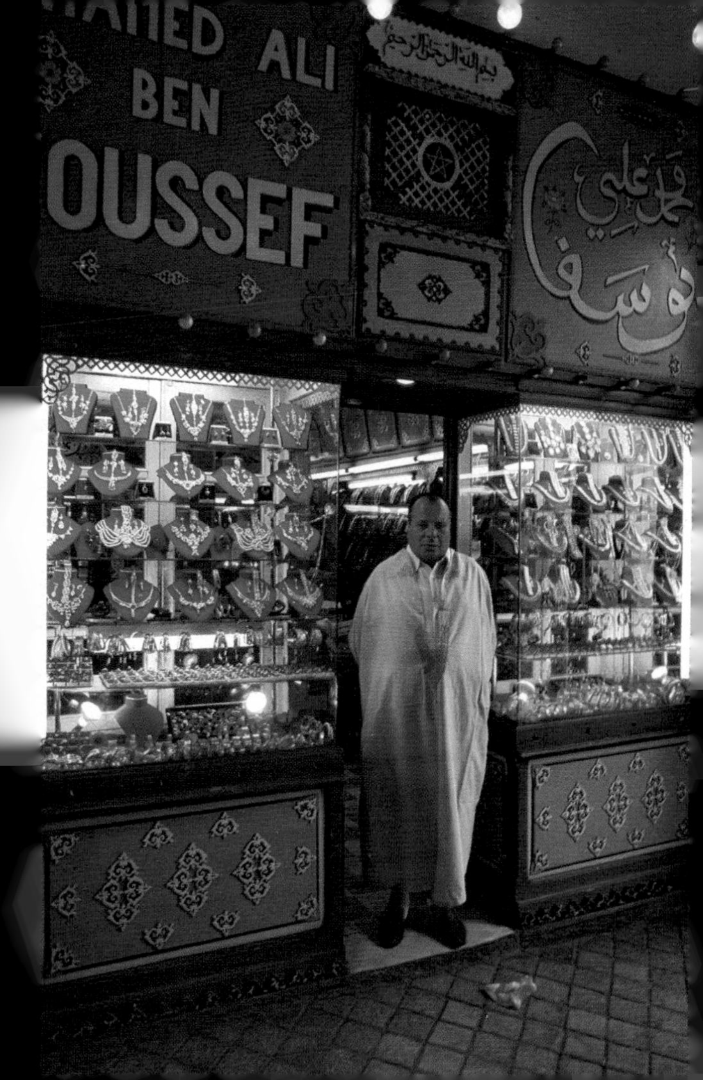

ALI
BEN
OUSSEF
بسم الله الرحمن الرحيم

Zitouna, once contained the Museum of Islamic Art. Although this collection of coinage, illuminated Korans and other artefacts has been moved to the Bardo and replaced by offices of the National Institute of Archaeology, it is still worth peeking at the enclosed court where brilliant panels of coloured ceramic tile decorate the walls, and delicate filigree worked in plaster graces the arches and windows. Wherever

Tunisian boys earn pocket money by selling traditional nosegays. A fragrant bunch of jasmine blossoms can sweeten the whole afternoon.

the eye turns it finds endless delights.

The **mosque and tomb of Hammoûda Pacha** (1655) reveal a bit of Tunisian history. When Ottoman Turkish governors came to rule, they brought with them a slightly different form of Islam than that commonly practised in Tunisia. The Tunisians followed the Malikite rite, while the Turkish conquerors observed the Hanifite. Hammoûda Pacha gave his mosque a minaret built on an octagonal base rather than the square base common to the Maghreb, and put a gallery on top so that all would know his mosque was of the Hanifite rite. The dramatic black-and-white designs on the minaret, mosque, and also on Hammoûda Pacha's tomb introduced a bold, foreign element which makes this complex of buildings among the *médina's* most beautiful.

Just up the hillside from Hammoûda Pacha's mosque is the centre of Tunisia's foreign ministry. The **Dar el Bey** (Seat of the Bey) was for a time the palace of Tunisia's ruling prince. First constructed in the 17th century, it has been rebuilt many times since. The hundreds of rooms are occupied by government officials pecking away at typewriters or carrying stacks of yellowing files here and there. The stone portals are guarded by tall soldiers resplendent in scarlet tunics, gold epaulettes and white peaked hats.

In the southern reaches of the *médina*, the **Dar ben Abdallah** houses the city's Museum of Folklore and Popular Arts. Wandering through the many ornate courtyards with their Islamic and Italianate decoration is both an aesthetic and educational experience. Here it's easy to imagine what life was like when pirates returned from the seas with hoards of gold, jewels and slaves, and merchant princes got rich buying and selling booty and holding distinguished captives for ransom.

Carthage

The Carthaginians (Phoenicians) were the first to build a powerful state in this part of North Africa, and so Carthage is quite literally where it all began. Later held by Rome and the Vandals, embattled for centuries, the city was finally reduced to ruins towards the end of the 7th century. The material from the devastated area was used to construct Tunis, the new capital of the country, and by 894 Carthage's heyday was over for good. The ruins are **31**

now surrounded by suburban villas and houses. The delightful seaside location makes Carthage a very desirable place to live, and the electric train (T.G.M.) between Carthage and Tunis (station at the foot of Avenue Bourguiba, at the port) makes commuting easy.

If you leave the train at Carthage-Salammbô, a short walk from the station brings you to the *tophet* (place of sacrifice) of Tanit and Baal Hammon, where for centuries the Carthaginians killed thousands of their first-born sons and daughters. The hearts of the young victims were burnt on an altar, and the sacrificial remains buried in urns commemorated by engraved stone slabs (stelae).

The **National Museum of Carthage** *(Musée National de Carthage)*, is best reached by leaving the train at Carthage-Dermech or Carthage-Hannibal stations, then walking to the top of the nearby Byrsa hill.

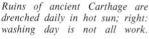

Ruins of ancient Carthage are drenched daily in hot sun; right: washing day is not all work.

The museum is in a handsome building with a façade of two arcades, one above the other, made with serpentine columns of creamy marble. Phoenician stelae, Roman sarcophagi, ancient items from ladies' toilettes, and statuary both Greek and Roman are in the museum's collection. Many other pieces are in the surrounding park among the cypress, pine and eucalyptus trees. Be careful in the park, for it's situated on unexcavated ruins. Deep pits, hollows, and various bits of rubble make it both fascinating and perilous to explore.

For a truly superb **view** of the ruins of Carthage, make your way up the spiral staircase to the roof of the former cathedral of St. Louis (1890). From here, in the pure and delicately **33** scented air, you can see the countryside all the way to Tunis.

Near the Carthage-Dermech, Carthage-Hannibal, or Carthage-Présidence stations are several other impressive ruins. The **Baths of Antoninus Pius** *(Thermes d'Antonin)*, built in the 2nd century were among the largest in the Roman Empire. In fact, "Baths" is almost inadequate to describe this immense pleasure palace of hundreds of rooms: cool rooms, warm rooms, and hot-steam rooms; rooms with pools and fountains, mosaics and frescoes; rooms for dining and rooms in which to have a massage from a comely youthful attendant. This was the social centre of a rich commercial city. A diagram chiselled into a slab of marble on a small observation platform will explain to you the various sections of the baths.

Up the slope from the baths is a lovely park filled with cascades of flowers, bits of interesting mosaics here and there, traces of ancient buildings, and wooded glades and thickets.

A short walk from this park, following the signs, brings you to the "Villas Romaines", a group of Roman ruins including the odeon and numerous hillside villas. One restored villa is used as a small museum to give a hint of what life was like here in ancient times. Many things have remained the same: the panorama of gentle green hills, the vivid sea, lizards clambering over pebbles and stones, a praying mantis motionless on a leaf. By the way, the massive seaside villa visible from here is the Carthage retreat of Tunisia's president.

The Roman theatre, at the base of the hill from the odeon has suffered much destruction since it was built in the 2nd century. Even worse, it has suffered much restoration. What you see is more an accomplishment of the 20th century than of the 2nd. No matter: on a lazy summer's evening during the Festival of Carthage, a Greek or Roman tragedy played here brings you close to the spirit of the theatre's ancient life.

Sidi Bou Saïd

Even before you go to Sidi Bou Saïd, near Carthage, you will have seen it. Posters of the storybook town are everywhere in Tunisia, and in lots of travel

Woodworkers' art is both elegant and functional: windows in Sidi Bou Saïd are "air-conditioned".

offices abroad. Sidi Bou Saïd is a cascade of sugar-cube houses, castles and minarets tumbled from the top of the hill down into the sea. The blue of sea and sky is matched by the wooden trim and window borders splashed with blue paint. The village is famous for its unspoiled beauty, for the pano-

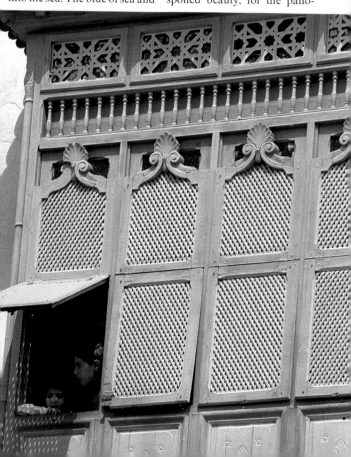

ramic view from the top of the hill (go all the way up to the lighthouse) and for the bulbous blue-and-white birdcages formed from an arabesque of wire and wood. The first such cages were made by a master craftsman from this village, and the ones still made here today are far superior to most imitations from other places.

The Bardo

The Bardo National Museum, once the fairytale palace of a renegade oriental monarch, now contains many of Tunisia's greatest treasures. Relics and artefacts from every period of the land's incredibly rich history are on display, and special attention has been given to the Roman mosaics for which the province of Africa was so justly famous. Plaster models of the major Punic and Roman archaeological sites in Tunisia show you where the discoveries were made. The rooms themselves are dazzling, decorated with thousands of tiles, pounds of gold leaf, mirrors, marble and ingeniously carved wood.

Sentries guarding one en-

White paint reflects the summer heat while blue trim brings to mind the coolness of the sea.

trance with swords at the ready add a dramatic touch: they protect the Majliss El Umma, or National Assembly, which meets in another wing of the palace.

Day-trip to Dougga

The Roman city of Thugga (today called Dougga) is one of the best-preserved in Africa. With a roof, its Capitol would be ready again for worshippers of Minerva, Jupiter and Juno. Its theatre is still adequate for dramatic performances during summer festivals. Streets and temples, forums and house foundations have all been uncovered in almost a century of archaeological excavations. Oddest and most mysterious of Dougga's remains is a Libyco-Punic **mausoleum** (3rd century B.C.), resembling early Armenian and Egyptian monuments, the only such mausoleum known to exist in this part of the world.

THUBURBO MAJUS, another Roman city about 60 km. (37 miles) from Tunis, is worth a visit if you're an avid archaeologist. So is SBEÏTLA (Sufetula), but its fascinating ruins are farther afield, almost 100 km. (62 miles) southwest of Kairouan. Organized excursions from Tunis are available to all of these Roman remains. **37**

Mysterious "Barbarians"

As far as anyone knows, there have always been Berbers in North Africa, from the Sahara to the Mediterranean coast, from Egypt to the Atlantic. Egyptian tomb paintings from 2,400 B.C. show costumes and people closely resembling the Berbers of today, and ancient inscriptions in Libya are in an alphabet very similar to one used by the Berbers. Theories abound concerning the origin of the people: various experts claim they can be traced to the Canaanites, Phoenicians, Celts or Basques. Although Berber dialects are still spoken, many have taken Arabic as their first language.

Berber tribes lived in both nomadic and settled fashion. But whether they travelled from oasis to oasis with their herds and flocks or whether they settled in small villages and towns to pursue agriculture, weaving and crafts, they always preserved a passion for independence from domination by "outsiders". Some say it was the Arabs, some say the Greeks, who first used the term "barbar" for people of uncouth manners and speech. In any case, the Berbers called themselves by other names and never used the word "Berber". Doubtless they had a different idea of who were "barbarians" and who were not.

Cap Bon Region

Hammamet

Whatever the Moslem warriors of the 12th century might have thought of Hammamet with its incomparably beautiful landscape and inviting beaches was of little consequence to the millionaire who "discovered" the town anew in the early 20th century. For him, and the few others who were in on the secret, it soon became an exclusive retreat in the sun.

Now, inexpensive air transport and well designed hotels make it possible for many people, wealthy or not, to enjoy this bit of paradise. Town planners have carefully avoided gigantism, and Hammamet's hostelries blend into the landscape, matching the traditional surroundings. The mansion built by that first millionaire is an international cultural centre, and has become a place for all to enjoy. Plays and concerts, lectures and exhibitions are held year-round, and they come as a relaxing change from the strenuous water sports. After the performance you can always wander down to the beach to think it over, picking oranges along the way. In Hammamet, the refreshments grow on trees.

The town is particularly clean and pretty, its white houses neatly arrayed along well-swept streets. Numerous restaurants, shops and cafés provide diversion for the casual stroller. At the southern end, on a point of land next to the *médina*, is the **kasba.** Garrisoned first by Moslem soldiers, and later by the French Foreign Legion, the little fort is interesting to visit. Nestling in its protective shadow are the narrow streets of the compact *médina.* Here, surprises are around every corner. Shopkeepers selling tourist souvenirs offer unbounded friendship if you'll take just one look in their shops. (Many of the most interesting items come from the hands of craftsmen in nearby Nabeul.)

What's in a Name?
Hammamet, when written in Arabic, could mean either "doves", or "bathing-places". If the sinuous curves and squiggles of written Arabic baffle you completely, it's comforting to know that even local people sometimes get confused. An old joke has it that in Arabic every word has three meanings: the original meaning, its exact opposite, and some part of a camel's anatomy. Believe it or not, there is some truth to the joke.

Nabeul
Nabeul is the handicrafts capital of Cap Bon. Ceramic work is king here, and all about town lattice-work lamps of baked clay advertise pottery shops. Piles of pots of every description fill shelves and courtyards. There are pots for oil and pots for water, pots for

flowers and pots just for fun. More serious as works of art are the dazzling panels of coloured tiles which are a Nabeul speciality. Designs on the large panels are usually traditional, such as two spindly cypress trees, or a lavishly coloured pot filled with stylized flowers, surrounded by a patterned border.

If a panel catches your eye and won't let go, remember that they can be taken apart into individual tiles for shipment. Reassembled at home as the top on a low table, or as the

A perfect place to be: on a beach, near flowers, friends and sea.

centre-piece of a tiled terrace, they'll provide a colourful and lasting souvenir.

Pottery is so much a part of Nabeul that even the town's symbol—albeit unofficial—is a giant evergreen tree growing in a pot. (If you look closely, you'll notice that the tree in fact grows from the ground through the pot.)

A walk through town reveals other craftsmen weaving fine grass mats. These are a popular way to decorate inexpensively and are often hung on walls and pillars in mosques and private houses. Lucky Nabeul belles can also have cloth embroidered with silver and gold. Simple dresses need only a narrow border of such wizardry to turn them into elegant gowns for evening wear. Be sure to take a turn through the fixed-price **Artisanat** (handicraft shop) to see the range and quality of local products before you do any serious buying.

Around and About the Cape

Wherever you go in Cap Bon, the greenery—citrus and olive trees, vineyards and flower gardens—will raise your spirits and delight your senses. There are also plenty of surprises for those willing to explore. The remains of the 5th-century settlement at KERKOUANE are said to be the best-preserved of any Punic village. At SIDI DAOUD and the ÎLE DE ZEMBRA you can watch the tunny fishermen make mass catches between May and July in a ceremony that dates back hundreds of years. Test your skill in a hunt for wild boar in the forests near KORBOUS. Visit the spa at AÏN OKTOR for a cure, or just for a few glasses of the healthful water. If you crave a more spirited drink, try the curious white wine called *Muscat Sec de Kélibia* right where it is produced, in the town of KÉLIBIA. Light and dry, but also somewhat sweet, it's uniquely Tunisian. Should you come to Cap Bon in May, try to visit the annual Festival of Falconry at EL HAOUARIA.

The Sahel

Centred on the cities of Sousse and Monastir, the Sahel (seacoast) draws thousands of tourists every year, and no wonder: the cities boast tempting beaches, good hotels and romantic castles in a pleasant Mediterranean environment. The surrounding countryside is a pretty patchwork of olive groves, fields of grain and flocks of contented sheep. The villages scattered throughout the district specialize in cloth-making, embroidery and the crafting of jewellery. In addition, a tourist coming to the Sahel finds the ancient towns of Kairouan and El Djem within easy range for a comfortable day excursion.

Sousse
(Pop. 100,000)
The capital of the Tunisian Sahel, Sousse is one of Tunisia's larger cities (third in size after Tunis and Sfax). Though it's a major port and a busy centre of industry and commerce, the bustle is on a Tunisian scale, and the relaxed atmosphere in the many beachfront hotels is hardly affected by it.

Hotels dot the waterfront, starting at the centre of town and extending northwards for several miles. Many are new and very well appointed, and all share in the vivid blue and sprightly sparkle of the Mediterranean waters.

Sousse's main boulevard is **Avenue Habib Bourguiba,** a microcosm of the city's life. Beginning at the end of the hotel zone, the avenue is lined by shops and restaurants, side-walk cafés and government offices, hotels and cinemas all the way to the port. As it nears the docks, the avenue touches

the rust-coloured walls of the *médina* which surround the city's most impressive historical monuments.

Attacked or defended for centuries, by Carthaginians, Romans, Vandals and Byzantines, Sousse finally succumbed to the redoubtable Oqba ibn Nafi, conqueror of Ifriqiya. The citizens held out for two months, but when the inevitable fall of the city arrived, Oqba's forces plundered it all the more savagely because of its stout resistance. Most traces of early buildings disappeared then, so that today Sousse can boast of a fine collection of Moslem monuments but few Roman and Punic buildings. Luckily, many priceless mosaics survived and are now on view in the museum.

Just off Place Farhat Hached is a convenient entrance to the **médina** of Sousse. Be sure to explore the old town between 8 a.m. and 2 p.m., when visits are permitted to the courtyard of the **Grand Mosque** (9th century). Surrounded by a harmonious arcade, the courtyard is paved in bright marble which contrasts sharply with the cool, quiet darkness of the prayer room (Moslems only, please!).

One of a Moslem's most important religious duties is that of charity. The handicapped **43** and disadvantaged may gather at the door to the mosque, asking for alms. There is no shame felt either by donor or recipient, as Moslems are supposed to help one another. The method is a good one, and the usual gift is only a coin or two—an insignificant amount to each donor, but many such contributions can make up a tidy sum.

Next to the Grand Mosque is the **ribat.** This 9th-century fortified monastery was the medieval home for a community of devout Moslems who held to a knightly code of conduct. Piety and bravery were the two pillars of the order, and one had to be as zealous in battle with infidels as one was humble in prayer. For a small admission fee visitors are allowed to clamber about the chambers and battlements, even to climb the claustrophobic spiral staircase to the top of the look-out minaret. The panoramic **view** from this man-made pinnacle is worth the climb. On your way out, check on evening entertainments currently being held in the *ribat.* A theatrical or folklore show here is just the thing to make medieval times come alive.

Stroll along the *médina's* Rue d'Angleterre to the *souks* for a look at local wares and handicrafts, then turn right and climb to the **kasba** and the adjoining Tour Khalaf once a signal tower. The **museum** in the *kasba* has a fine collection of mosaics, as in most Tunisian museums. Just past the inner door, a huge head of Medusa lies in wait for the unwary visitor: legend has it that a glimpse of this snake-haired lady turned a mortal to stone —especially a mortal hairdresser—but today the face on the museum floor is more likely to inspire wonder at the artistry and workmanship of the Romans.

Next, several rooms of mosaics open onto a lovely flower garden with a shady trellis and numerous fragments of statuary. The gigantic mosaic of a lion is fearfully realistic, and another enormous work gives a glimpse of Roman life: the scene is an amphitheatre, where four dauntless hunters pit themselves against a pack of panthers. An inscription explains that this sport was organized and paid for by a patrician named Magerius. His servant is pictured holding a tray loaded with bags of money, a thousand *denarii* for each of the fearless huntsmen.

For the best-ever **view** of Sousse, climb the stairway from the garden to the ledge at the top of the *kasba* wall.

Monastir

Smaller and sleepier than Sousse, Monastir might be termed that city's younger sister. Just as in real life, younger sisters are sometimes the prettier ones. The sinuous coastline conceals small, sandy coves, often protected by low cliffs and hills which rise out of the water. A fine **promenade** winds around one such cove just at the foot of the hill crowned by Monastir's redoubtable *ribat*. All the things

Young merchant tends the shop at prayer-time. Coloured yarn will soon be a Tunisian carpet.

you'll want to see are within easy reach of this landmark.

Start with the **ribat** itself. The imposing fortress-monastery, dating from the 11th century, dominates the harbour and the town. One can almost see, amid the complexity of crenellated walls and turrets, open courtyards and spartan cells, the men who lived and died here in accordance with their ascetic vows. Many an attacking Christian fleet must have been beaten back from here by the mighty guns of the town's medieval defenders. But not one of them remains today, and the wanderer is left to do the range-finding with his imagination. Next to the *ribat*, the simple but venerable **Grand Mosque** (11th century) has been well-restored and modernized to the point of having a crackly loudspeaker for calling the faithful to prayer.

More than for its ancient monuments, Monastir is famous among Tunisian cities as the birthplace of the republican hero, President Habib Bourguiba (born 1903). Successful beyond his family's wildest dreams, this son of Monastir resides in a presidential mansion at Skanès when he comes to visit. The **Bourguiba Mosque** near the *ribat* was erected in the family's honour and though not ancient (it was built in 1963) its harmonious design and the lavish use of rich, attractive materials make it a place to admire. Features have been borrowed from all periods of Tunisian architecture. The sumptuous main portal is used only for very special occasions. Walk around to the entrance at the base of the minaret, and take a peek at the courtyard through the iron-grilled windows.

Kairouan

Alone on a desert plain, bright and dusty and great with age, stands Kairouan. No trip to Tunisia is complete without an excursion to this citadel of Islam. Buses leave Tunis approximately every hour for the two-hour bus-trip to Kairouan; or you could take an organized tour.

Kairouan is a place of tremendous historical significance for the whole Arab world. Built from the ground up on bare steppe in 671, it was uncontaminated by any pagan or infidel past. As the capital of the Maghreb it was made to be an Islamic stronghold forever.

"Barber's Mosque" in Kairouan: renowned for richness of decoration.

46

The walls of the *kasba* were certain to hold off all adversaries.

The city's most famous and venerable sight, the **Grand Mosque,** is itself a virtual fortress with high walls and strong, defendable gates. Under the circumstances, one might expect that such a holy spot would be fiercely defended against intrusion by infidel tourists, but the good citizens of Kairouan have opened their cherished monument to interested visitors. The Syndicat d'Initiative (tourist office) will issue you a permit for a small fee.

In its present form the Grand Mosque dates from the 9th century. Visitors are allowed to inspect the great courtyard, surrounded by a colonnade and paved in marble, but the gleaming tiles of the *mihrab* (prayer niche) and the thicket of rich marble and porphyry columns in the prayer room are not open to anyone but devout Moslems. Be sure to stroll along the perimeter of the mosque after your visit to the interior. The Gate of Lalla Rihana, in the eastern wall, is the prettiest of the many portals.

Across the street from the entrance to the Grand Mosque is the small museum of Ibrahim ibn el Aghlab, with artefacts from Kairouan's Islamic past.

Other mosques worthy of attention are the **zaouïa of Sidi Sahab,** also called the "Barber's Mosque". It's noted for its handsome decorative tiles. Sidi Sahab was a personal friend of Mohammed's and so his final resting place is very sacred to Moslems, but you can visit it, using the same permit as for the Grand Mosque. Then there's the ancient **Djamâ Tleta Bibane** (Mosque of the Three Doors); not far from the centre of the city, it dates back to the 9th century.

Wandering around, Kairouan's sights grow more and more curious. Incongruous with the desert setting, large pools of limpid water prove to be open-air reservoirs built by the Aghlabid governors who did so much to embellish Kairouan in the 9th century. Later advances in aqua-mechanics helped to provide the city with water in a trusty if unique way: the Bir Barouta (Well of Barouta), inside a small, inconspicuous building in the market, is driven by a blindfolded camel. The one-camel-power pump has been in operation for almost three centuries.

For all its hoary antiquity and its importance as a Moslem sanctuary, Kairouan has a vibrant modern side as well. A walk within the old city walls takes one through *souks* festooned with Kairouan carpets, famous throughout Tunisia for their special patterns and colours. Every other doorway is filled with women making the carpets on primitive looms, and street-corner marketplaces are piled with gaily coloured skeins of wool—the raw material of the carpetweavers. Just outside the Bab Tounes (Tunis gate), a potter's yard displays water and oil jugs, amphorae, tremendous vessels and even tiny pots made so that Kairouan's young girls can "play house". When they grow up, and Kairouan's maidens set up house for real, the wedding is a lively happening: a caravan of the ubiquitous Peugeot diesel cars and vans, laden with dowry, trousseau, musicians and relatives takes the bride to her new house. A small native band hoots noisily from the back of a van. At the end of the procession a Health Department vehicle has been pressed into service because its musical klaxon can toot out an unexpected few bars of "Here Comes the Bride".

For a desert city, Kairouan abounds in a surprising number of good things to nibble on. Fruit stands in the *souks* bear heavy loads of oranges, dates, figs, raisins, and pomegranates.

Some of the busiest shops are those which sell the famous diamond-shaped confections called *maqroudh*, made of semolina saturated with syrup and filled with date paste. A half-dozen of these desert desserts should cost less than 200 Millimes. The fastest way to draw a crowd in Kairouan is to buy a kilo of *maqroudh* and give one to every passing child who greets you with a gay *"bonjourr"*—they all do!

El Djem

Approaching El Djem by road leaves little doubt as to the town's main attraction. The **Roman amphitheatre** (3rd century) rises right in the middle of the arrow-straight highway, surrounded by the modern town. From whichever direction you approach it, the amphitheatre is a tremendously impressive sight. One of the largest in the Roman world, the great circus has been the scene of many a game and battle. Rebels throughout the centuries found it an excellent substitute for a fortress. In fact, so often was it used as a stronghold for armies of malcontents that one Turkish bey had part of it dismantled in the late 17th century. His work, destructive as it was, benefits the visitor today, for now it's easy to see **49**

every detail of the intricate building. Arches, stairways, seats, buttresses and underground rooms are all on view.

Under the Romans El Djem was a lively and prosperous town almost four times as large as the modern one. Evidence of its wealth can still be seen in the striking mosaics in the small **museum** at the edge of town on the road south. Seashells and birds, lions, tigers, and peacocks are all beautifully formed with the brightly coloured bits of stone. A large mosaic of the young Dionysos, dressed in a leopard skin and mounted on a tigress, is especially impressive. The collection is particularly rich in mosaics done in geometric designs, curlicue patterns, and stylized plants and flowers.

South of El Djem lies SFAX, Tunisia's second-largest city (after Tunis) and an important industrial and commercial centre. Good for a quick lunch en route or an emergency stop overnight. Sfax holds little to delay tourists rushing south to the delights of Djerba or the mysteries of the Tunisian desert.

With no shop to maintain, this carpet seller offers bargain prices.

► Djerba

(Pop. 65,000)

Imagine a flat landscape, sandy and somewhat dry, but well covered with ancient olive trees, fruit trees, palms and grasses; little white houses topped by hemispherical domes, each house with its own private courtyard; men and women in straw hats; camels pulling the plough. Soon, one realizes that Djerba is unlike the rest of Tunisia in many ways. More slowly, it becomes clear that Djerba is like nowhere else in the world.

Djerba owes its peculiarities and beauties to its location. Deep in the southern part of Tunisia, not far from the border with Libya, the tiny island rests like a refuge in the warm waters off the Tunisian coast. This African paradise is almost completely flat and, except for a few rocky places, is bordered by beautiful sandy beach.

The fact that Djerba now has its own modern airport for large jets, and an outstanding assortment of luxurious hotels, doesn't seem to bother the local people. After all, tourists who come are looking for the same things that Djerbans themselves enjoy: sunny days, an easy pace, sea breezes, plus a sense of being special and separate from the rest of the world. It's just these things which have kept the island a special place over the centuries.

Access to Djerba by car is easy, whether you drive all the way using the long causeway from Zarzis or take the short ferry ride from Djorf to Adjim. Whichever way you arrive, it won't take you long to get the lie of the land, for the island is less than 25 miles from shore to shore at its widest point. Tourist activity is centred in the Zone Hôtelière (Resort Hotel Area) on the eastern side of the island. The fine beaches on either side of Cap Tourgueness are dotted with large hotels equipped with all the services and pleasures one might desire. The atmosphere is friendly and visitors move freely from one hotel to another enjoying activities wherever they may find them, just as though the entire area were one grand holiday village.

The beaches—**Sidi Maharès, Sidi Garous** and **La Séguia**— stretch for about 12 miles, interrupted only by the rocks of **Cap Tourgueness.** The cape, by the way, is the best place on the island for scuba diving, snorkelling and spear-fishing. The possibilities for daytime fun seem endless. Ride a horse or a camel, sail with a gentle breeze **51** or row in the easy-moving surf, play a few games of ping-pong at the poolside, or take part in a volleyball match for exercise and to meet new friends. Bicycles and horse-drawn carriages with comfortable suspension are for hire at all hotels.

Djerban Genie

One room of Djerba's museum, known as *koubet el Khiâl* (Dome of the Phantoms), is said to be the burial place of the *zaouïa's* saintly former monk, Sidi Zitouni. Legend has it that devout Moslem men used to visit this domed room so they could be married to a genie. The prospective bridegroom would stay in the lonely, shadowy room all night reading the Koran and praying for the saint's intercession with some young genie maiden. All night ghosts and phantoms would whirl around the suitor, trying to distract him from his devotions, but if he had the strength and courage to disregard them, his genie bride would appear just at dawn.

The children born of this unearthly wedlock would live in the world of men, not in the spirit world, but they would be invisible—neither seen, nor heard. Unfortunately, no population statistics of these well-behaved little genii have been kept.

Djerban Traditions

For centuries men have lived happily on Djerba, ploughing its sandy soil and hauling up water from its brackish wells. Farming here is hard work, but the climate is mild, and the island has another important attraction: religious freedom. When the rulers in Carthage, Kairouan or Tunis demanded obedience to the official religion, dissenters and heretics would flee to the solitude of this island in order to live and worship as they liked. Even today, most Djerbans are Kharijites (unorthodox Moslems) with their own particular mosques and customs. Djerba is also the home of a sizeable Jewish congregation who built their synagogue here when they fled from Jerusalem after the holy city's destruction by Nebuchadnezzar in the 6th century B.C.

Separation from the mainland has given Djerba a unique culture. It's not common to see men and women in straw hats in mainland Tunisia, but in Djerba everyone sports a sunbonnet, and its particular shape and style shows which island

Djerba is full of things to do: but poolside sunning can sometimes monopolize an entire day.

village the wearer comes from.

In the evening, the choice of activities is no less tantalizing, for many hotels have their own nightclubs and discotheques, cosy bars and outdoor barbecues. Each hotel sponsors an evening of folklore once a week when Tunisian musicians provide the background for a Ber-ber damsel's "Dance of the Seven Veils" and other exotic entertainments. The one night-time diversion which no one misses on Djerba is a quiet walk on the beach. The gentle washing of the waves, the moon and stars clear in the cool and fragrant night air will be a memory you won't forget.

Houmt Souk

Houmt Souk is the business centre of the island, with airline offices, banks, travel agencies, car rental firms, and many small shops. Start your explorations at the small but very fine Museum of Folklore and Popular Arts *(Musée des Arts et Traditions Populaires)*, on the

Handprint wards off evil eye from geometric mosque in Midoun. Above: Guellala artist at work.

road to the hotel area at the edge of town. The ancient *zaouïa* of Sidi Zitouni, set in a pretty garden, has been converted to hold fascinating **55** exhibits from Djerba's everyday life. Antique jewellery, pottery (plain and fancy), joinery and woodcarving show the careful work of local craftsmen, and manuscript Korans are testaments to their devotion. The *zaouïa* itself is a maze of tiny rooms, one with a fine filigreed plaster ceiling, others with decorative tiles. The museum is open every day except Friday.

Houmt Souk's outstanding medieval monument is the fortress of **Bordj el Kébir** (Great Fort), north of the town on the seacoast. A work of the 15th century (recently restored), it was garrisoned in its time by Hafsids, Spaniards and Turks.

After the Turkish corsairs stormed the fort in 1560, its stubborn defenders were put to the sword—such were the rules of war. A tall pyramid was built with their skulls. No doubt this grisly monument caused more perspiration than inspiration among the remaining Djerbans.

The **centre** of Houmt Souk is a delightful place for a stroll. The warren of *souks*, both covered and uncovered, and the several market squares are

Take your pick: Houmt Souk shops are filled with good buys such as these brilliant copper pots.

packed with a bewildering assortment of treasures and souvenirs. Several of the narrow streets have shops specializing in carpets, or jewellery, or leather, but most shops have a variety of goods, from embroidered caftans and shirts to baskets and bird cages. If the choice of goods seems overwhelming, a number of town squares are furnished with café tables where you can sit quietly, sip something refreshing and take it all in at your leisure.

Most of the *souks* are on the well-trodden tourist path. Other markets are more typically Djerban. At the municipal market *(marché municipal)*, the National Fisheries Office *(Office National des Pêches)* occupies a large stall, and each afternoon the day's catch is auctioned off to the highest bidder from restaurant or household. With some drama and bravado, the auctioneer will scoop up a juicy octopus, point triumphantly to a huge section of tunny or hold tenderly a shimmering *daurade* (sea bream) while the buyers jealously compete with each other. Gaily coloured tile panels depicting nautical scenes provide a suitable backdrop. Here and there in the market you'll see other curiosities such as the barrel-shaped pieces of granite with many lengthwise grooves, once used in a primitive mill or olive press.

Other Island Sights

Five miles south of Houmt Souk is the island's oldest house of worship, the venerable synagogue called **La Ghriba.** The route is tricky—turn from the main road and follow the sign for ERIADH, and then in that village look for signs to La Ghriba (or El Graiba/El Gariba). The synagogue and adjoining monastery and hostel form two large, squarish buildings painted white and bedecked with Tunisian flags which give them the appearance of government offices. A wizened sage with a twinkle in his eye is your host, and he will lead you through the large sanctuary, ablaze with hundreds of tiles, to the inner sanctum. You will be asked to remove your shoes and to cover your head before you enter. This is the oldest part of the synagogue and may have foundations dating from about 550 B.C. Of the priceless Torahs preserved here, one is said to be among the oldest in the world.

Guellala, on the southern side of the island and about 18 km. (12 miles) from Houmt Souk, is Djerba's pottery **57**

centre. Crowding the village's bumpy, unpaved streets are dozens of small potters' workshops, kilns and factories, each with its small sign inviting tourists to come in and have a look. Pots of all descriptions can be bought or made to order, but the artisans of Guellala don't stop there. All sorts of household utensils and ornaments are crafted from the pliant clay, and only the master's imagination limits the assortment of fanciful and useful items. Pottery is Guellala's livelihood, and broken or spoiled pots are a natural resource. Fences, backyard ovens, kilns and even small sheds and cabins are made from chipped or broken pots. The only exception to this "pots for everything" rule is in headgear. You can always tell a Guellala girl by her tall, pointed "Greek-style" straw hat.

Djerba's second-biggest town, **Midoun,** is reminiscent of Houmt Souk in many respects. Shops line its clean and cheery streets, a municipal market is fragrant with fruit and vegetables, and pensive old men inhabit customary chairs in customary cafés. Midoun is a convenient place to pick up a souvenir, have a meal, buy medicine or suntan lotion, or get a clock repaired. Come on Friday to join in the action of the weekly market.

In MAHBOUBINE, the many backyard gardens are among Djerba's most varied and "fruitful". Apples, apricots, citrus fruits, figs, grapes, olives and almonds are all found here. Most of the many plots and orchards are hidden behind forbidding walls of tall cactus to keep out predators, both two- and four-legged.

Zarzis

Though Djerba has always been a tempting resort, Zarzis is a newcomer to the field. A large oasis surrounds the modern town and serves as a backdrop for several miles of perfect beach. The hotel area extends along the length of the sand, with hostelries large and small built among the palm groves or nestling in the green hills which border the beach. Many of the hotels here are even newer than those on Djerba and offer the same wide range of services and activities. As for sun, sand and sea, Zarzis has enough to satisfy even the most demanding appetite.

Backed by a huge pot, Guellala maiden shows off handwoven material of her traditional costume.

Southern Tunisia and the Desert

To journey into the desert is to catch a glimpse of man's indefatigable spirit. Shifting sands, burning and blowing across infinite spaces, is very often the conception of the Sahara, and it's partly true, for there are many such places in the desert. But there are other parts where people have learned to carry on life in special ways suited to the inhospitable climate.

A map of the desert reveals a vast area with mountains, valleys and salt flats. Life centres around the scattered oases and isolated wells discovered and exploited over the centuries by men determined to conquer the wasteland. But some places just couldn't be made fit to live in. Such a place is the arid CHOTT EL DJÉRID, the largest of the Sahara's salt lakes, with an area of almost 2,000 square miles. To the west and south of the *chott* are the *ergs*, limitless expanses of sand dunes, untamed and unrelieved, constantly moving, defeating and burying all who venture in unprepared.

Kébili, Douz, Tozeur and Nefta can all be reached by good roads either on an excursion organized by your hotel, or by rented car. Tozeur has recently acquired its own airport, due one day to handle international traffic. But for the *ksars* and *ghorfas* of the far south, it's advisable to take a tour by Land-Rover or bus, unless you're prepared to rent an overland vehicle, a guide and emergency equipment. It can be done, but it's expensive...

Ksars and Ghorfas

The people of Tunisia's far south remain true to their Berber origins. Though many are settled in villages, others maintain the nomadic ways of their ancestors. In the 11th century when the Arabic tribe of the Beni Hilal overran Tunisia from Egypt and Libya, the Berbers retreated to the hills and built homes, granaries and fortresses. These settlements have changed little since then, and though some are now deserted, others are very much alive.

You'll need to know a few exotic words to understand life in the far south. A *ghorfa* is a Berber granary, a long rectangular room topped by a semicylindrical roof. Very often *ghorfas* are built on top of one another, and beehive-like complexes of three and four levels are not unusual. Such *ghorfas* built around a rectangular

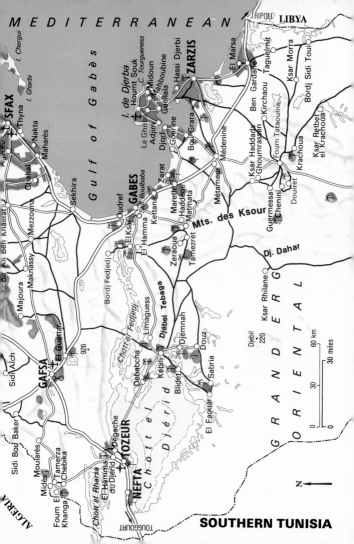

SOUTHERN TUNISIA

open court form a *ksar*.* In times of peace, villagers who own *ghorfas* in the *ksar* gather here to gossip and take the air, or play host to the weekly market. In times of unrest, people flock to the *ksar* for refuge because its fortress-like formation is easy to defend. If this fails, the community's last bastion is a *kalaâ*, or citadel, built in a commanding position above the town. No one actually lived in the *ghorfas*, *ksars* or *kalaâs* of times past, though nearby houses often resembled these structures.

Outstanding examples of these intriguing Berber settlements are dotted across the south of Tunisia. The busy city of **Médenine** was once a major grain depot and held a honeycomb of 6,000 *ghorfas*. Today only a few dozen are left, grouped around three courtyards, but they're enough to build an image of Médenine's lively past. On the outskirts of the city, the village of **Métameur's** *ghorfas* are even more picturesque.

To get the feeling of what life was like in the isolated Berber strongholds, head south through Foum Tataouine to the mountain *ksars*. Chenini is

a small village glued to the side of a mountain. A tiny mosque painted white will draw your attention, but the rest of the village's buildings seem almost to disappear into the rock itself. Fashioned from the same stone, they provided the best possible camouflage against the marauders from the valleys below. Though many of its houses and *ghorfas* are in ruins, Chenini is still inhabited. Archaeologists come here to puzzle over the giant tombs

---

* The plural of *ksar* in Arabic is pronounced *ksour*.

Ghorfas *for grain storage enclose a central courtyard, making a* ksar. *In wartime it's a fortress, in peacetime the village marketplace.*

near the mosque, unmarked and mysterious.

At DOUIRET, the *ksars* and *kalaâ* are ranged along several mountain peaks. Some of the *ghorfas* are kept in good repair, and the dwellings used by the villagers look like converted *ghorfas*, with the family living on the ground floor and grain being stored—hauled up by the bucketful—in the top-floor chamber. Many houses have "spare rooms" at the rear, hollowed right out of the mountain.

The challenge of GUERMESSA is to scramble up the narrow path from the village to the *kalaâ*, an aerie perched high above town and accessible only by a narrow, rocky path. When **63**

you finally come panting to the top, the panorama is a fitting reward.

GHOUMRASSEN is a town both old and new. In the older part, long rows of houses are nestled into the cliff, and almost qualify as troglodyte dwellings.

IN KSAR HADDADA, you'll have the opportunity to find out at first-hand how the Berbers lived: the National Tourism Office has converted a number of *ghorfas* into a *marhala* (inn), a welcome and fitting overnight rest-stop on your desert expedition.

Oases

"A plot of paradise in the midst of an inferno"—that is a desert dweller's definition of an oasis. Surrounded by a landscape of barren rock and sand, blazing in the daytime, chilling at night, the oasis is much more than just a watering place. Painstaking and meticulous labour, plus a good measure of ingenuity and inspiration, are necessary to make the desert bloom. A rare well or rivulet is coaxed and cultivated, the bottom-land is expanded and enriched, and

Something worth waiting for: a desert rest-stop just before sunset.

eventually the palm grove, which is essential for shade, grows in size. Soon the oasis-dweller's meagre diet of dates and camel's milk can be augmented with grain, figs, apricots and a few root vegetables. Finally, the oasis becomes a well-irrigated, almost tropical garden paradise producing a full range of fruits, vegetables, fodder and ornamental flowers.

The garden is the heart and life of the oasis village. All refuse, including camel dung, is ploughed back into the soil so that nothing is lost. Too valuable to be covered with houses, every inch of the shaded, moist earth is used for cultivation, and houses must be built on higher land, even if they are in the merciless sun.

The Tunisian south is strewn with oases of all sizes and characters, from the great jungle-like oasis of Gabès to the typical, small oasis of Nefta. A tour of the south would not be complete without a visit to one of these cool palm forests. Frequent excursions are organized from Djerba and Zarzis, and expeditions from northern resorts are not uncommon. Because many oases are served by good paved roads, a do-it-yourself tour by rented car is also possible.

Gabès

A seaside oasis might be the most exotic sight in the world, but in busy Gabès, people take it in their stride. Gabès is a large town, known as the "Gateway to the South" because all highway traffic from north to south must pass through it. Shops, government offices, and a resort complex make the modern town seem much like any other along the Tunisian coast. But in the very large oasis, right next to the modern town, life reverts to an earlier time.

The Gabès oasis is so big that a dozen separate villages are hidden in its shady depths, and a serpentine road penetrates it to link them together. The most delightful way to tour this forest of 300,000 palms is by *calèche* (horse-drawn carriage). Start at the National Tourist Office, where you can hire one at the official, fixed rate, and then clip-clop along the shady road past well-irrigated gardens. Each plot is surrounded by a fence of palm fronds to keep out marauding goats and misguided children. Your driver-guide will take you to see the handicraft products of Chenini village.

If you have an extra hour or two when you return to the modern town, drop in at the Handicrafts Centre (*centre artisanal*) to see Gabès craftsmen at work on carpets and baskets. The Museum of Folklore and Popular Arts, in the Sidi Boulbaba mosque, is also worth visiting to acquaint you with many aspects of daily life in the Tunisian south.

Matmata

In the rocky, dramatic range of the Matmata foothills lies Tunisia's most curious village, also named Matmata. The Matmatans are Berbers, and they work diligently to glean a livelihood from the dry soil. Olive trees are scattered throughout the valley, and here and there the big leaves of a fig tree or elongated fronds of a palm throw a little shade on the dusty earth. But as you approach the village, driving over a ridge and descending to the valley floor, it's soon obvious what makes Matmata special: the valley floor is a moonscape of craters, hollowed out of the soft rock, and in the walls of the craters men have made their dwellings.

The way things were—and still are—at the lush oasis of Gabès.

At first it all seems rather strange, but on reflection one can imagine, many years ago, the first Matmatan coming upon the practical idea of cutting dwellings out of the rock. First they dug craters and convenient entrance tunnels, then hollowed out homes, granaries, stables, tool rooms, storage rooms and even rooms big enough for a camel-driven olive press. The cool and pleasant temperature inside is much the same, winter and summer. If he feels the need for an extra room or some shelves or perhaps a pit to store oil, a Matmatan home-owner just gets out his chisel and mallet, hammers away, sweeps out the dust and *voilà!* the new "addition" (actually, it's more of a "subtraction").

The discovery of Matmata by the outside world has added a new element to the tenuous local economy. Restaurants, souvenir shops, and men offering camel rides all help to keep Matmata prosperous. Two hotels have been established in disused craters. The rooms are troglodytic, but the plumbing, lighting and other facilities are definitely 20th-century. By spending the night here, or just by visiting a hotel for a few minutes, tourists can examine Matmata's fascinating under-ground "apartment buildings" without disturbing the local folk in their homes.

Kébili and Douz

Nothing can match the excitement of speeding along the fast paved road from Gabès to the oases of Kébili and Douz, near the shores of the Chott el Djérid and the dunes of the Grand Erg Oriental. At EL HAMMA are hot sulphur baths once used by the Romans. To the north lies the salt lake of Chott el Fedjedj, and to the south the dusty summits of the Djébel Tebaga mountains.

Kébili, on the border of the Chott el Djérid, is an oasis surrounded by sand. Two picturesque old desert strongholds have been converted to hotel-restaurants, and guests dine and slumber among the ghosts of the Foreign Legion garrison. Until barely over a century ago, Kébili was a notorious market for slaves brought up from the south.

Past Kébili the great dunes rise. Many are formed as the wind-blown sand catches on fences put up to keep the highway from being covered. The hamlet of DJEMNAH, half way from Kébili to Douz, is a picturebook oasis: young girls walk home from the well with water jars on their shoulders, and camel caravans rest in the sun while their loads are packed up.

Surrounded by dunes, **Douz** allows itself the luxury of an entrance road bordered by fragrant eucalyptus trees. When you emerge from your car, it's a surprise to find the desert air so marvellously light and pure. Douz reveals itself at once. Some houses and official buildings are painted white, but most are sand-coloured, and except for the main street, all the roads are sand tracks. In the courtyard of each private home the family vehicle is parked, awaiting the next trip into the desert—it is rarely a normal car, sometimes a Land-Rover, most often a trusty camel.

On Thursdays the town is at its busiest, for that is when the semi-nomadic tribesmen from small surrounding oases come to market. The market square is filled with men in brown burnouses and white head-cloths haggling over sacks of wool, piles of beans, fruits and vegetables, bundles of fodder, stacks of new and used clothing. Cafés are crowded, the tiny local bakery turns out dozens upon dozens of fresh hot loaves, and everyone joins in the weekly festivities.

The desert **camel market** is a festival in itself as buyers and sellers haggle next to the long-suffering beasts. "How is it possible", the buyer asks, "that this poor decrepit thing can be offered for sale? I would not give the husk of a fig…" The seller, awestruck by this effrontery, insists that the beast is barely out of the womb, that it is not even yet in its prime. "Disease is a thing foreign to it, as God is my witness!" The camel may voice its opinion with a raucous roar, and this sign of life is used by both antagonists as a bargaining point. No used car lot in the world could see as much spirited bargaining or hear as many ingenious arguments as the camel market in Douz.

In December Douz comes alive with the **Festival of the Sahara.** Shooting contests, traditional ceremonies and plays, and camel fights fill the days and nights of a week. Poets declaim in a *joute poétique* (poetical "jousting match"). Horsemen gather from the surrounding regions to stage a *fantasia*—a mock charge full of excitement as the horses come thundering down on the audience, driven on by gunfire and war-cries, only to turn and retreat at the last possible moment, leaving the "attacked" audience breathless.

Gafsa, Tozeur and Nefta

In the middle of Tunisia's phosphate-producing area, **Gafsa** is a city of bureaucrats, quarry-workers and small businessmen. Roads from north and south meet in Gafsa before continuing west to Tozeur and Nefta. Stop for fuel or refreshment, find refuge in a hotel, seek out the ancient *kasba* or the Roman swimming pool *(piscine romaine)* for a quick dip. A tiny garden park in the centre of town is filled with jasmine and watched over by a bust of President Bourguiba. The town's oasis produces a variety of fruits and delicious nuts.

Tozeur marks the limits of Roman Africa. Its name comes from the Latin, Thusuros, and many a Roman legion would stop at its cool oasis on their way from Gabès to Nefta. The town is now the centre of the Djérid region, and is growing quickly. Cars and lorries rattle along its sandy streets, and

Desert souvenirs are hand-made.
Above: salt springs feed salt lakes.

television antennas poke up from the ochre-coloured houses of unbaked brick. But beyond this façade of modern prosperity, Tozeur still pursues its ancient traditions.

Many buildings exhibit the local talent for decorative bricklaying; shops, cafés and houses all bear interesting geometric designs done in this manner. Souvenir shops hang out colourful carpets and mats bearing stylized men and animals. The patterns are unique to the region and quite unusual for a Moslem town, as Islam forbids the portrayal of men and beasts in any form. Veiled women scuff down the sandy streets to the bustling produce market by the post office, while men and women from out of town bargain with shopkeepers for the famous *degla en-nour* ("radiant dates"). These deli- **71**

Finely decorated brickwork and a woman wearing a black shawl: lingering traditions in Tozeur.

ciously sweet, plump delicacies are sold by the branchful packed in large plastic bags, or by the kilo neatly packed in small wooden boxes.

The cafés in the town's main square do a flourishing business all day, but are best appreciated in the early morning and late evening when the air is exquisitely fresh and cool. During the hottest part of the day it's best to stay in the air-conditioned comfort of a hotel, or in a patch of shade at the swimming pool. Many tourists just visiting for the day escape to Tozeur's oasis, watered by a stream which springs hot from the earth at Ras el Aïoun and ripples along through the forest of 200,000 palm trees.

The road from Tozeur to Nefta passes the modern airport and enters increasingly dry and barren country. As you ride along a ridge approaching Nefta, the great salt lake of Chott el Djérid shimmers with intense heat and brilliant light, a limitless stage for the play of mirages. This is truly the edge of the Sahara.

No other Tunisian settlement fits so well the description of a desert oasis as **Nefta.** From the high ground which holds Nefta's houses, stores and mosques, one can peer down into a depression covered in palm trees and watered by countless springs. This *corbeille* (basket) of palms as it's known, shelters a lush and fragrant garden where the hot desert wind becomes a cool and soothing breeze, and the sound of trickling water is an unexpected delight. It's a surprise to see such abundance in the middle of the desert: dates, figs, bananas, peppers, pomegranates, vegetables and flowers lend their sweet fragrances to this bit of paradise. Even the word "oasis" takes on a new richness and importance when one has experienced the real thing.

Because of its many *marabouts* (saints' tombs) and mosques, Nefta has been a place of pilgrimage for many years. On religious holidays life in town is especially active, and no pilgrim who must answer to the folks back home dares forget to buy some Nefta dates to give as gifts.

Away From It All

If you've time for a side trip, the remote oases of Chebika, Tamerza and Midès are the most likely places to go. CHEBIKA's waters flow from a

red-rock gorge. At TAMERZA, the Oued Khanga forms a deep ravine to hold the town's houses and gardens, and there's even a waterfall. MIDÈS, at the end of a gorge, presents a fortress-like façade made all the more forbidding by its remote location.

The Far North

The northern coast of Tunisia is only about 95 miles from Sicily. The sea route from east to west passes through these straits, and sea traffic has made the region's history since the earliest times.

The Phoenicians stopped frequently along the coast and Utica was founded as their first way station in this region. The Romans made Bizerta *(Hippo Diarrhytus)* a prosperous port and later, with the coming of Islam, the northern shore took on a new role as part of the Barbary Coast. Christian merchantmen, low in the water with rich cargoes, dreaded this narrow sea channel for it was known to harbour bold and unpleasantly efficient Moslem pirates. The coast's many coves,

Family life "Berber style": a portable home, no cars, no television and plenty of sunshine. **75**

sheltered and hidden by rocky outcrops, were perfect places for a pirates' lair. The port towns had impressive fortifications, and their economies were designed to operate on other people's money. Even as late as 1963, Bizerta still held its important place as guardian of the sea roads, and France, which had special title to the city, gave it up only with great reluctance.

Modern industries now bring in the wealth once provided by brigands, and one such industry is based on a very old pursuit: diving for coral. The Direction des Pêches, Ministère de l'Agriculture (Ministry of Agriculture, Fisheries Department), issues permits for fishing and diving, and when you've obtained one of these, the Coral Coast and its underwater treasures are open to you. The ideal tourist here is the vagabond with fishing or diving gear and a car, prepared to exchange picturesque villages for secluded coves as the spirit moves him. Before donning mask and flippers for the first dive, take a quick look at Bizerta.

Bizerta *(Bizerte)*

After the French withdrawal in 1963, Bizerta changed from a busy military and naval post to an easygoing trade centre, modern in most respects but bearing vestiges of a fascinating past. The **vieux port** (old port) is the city's most alluring quarter. Small fishing boats bob and bump in the water as their owners sew nets or fill café chairs and speculate on tomorrow's catch. Bizerta's *kasba* and the hilltop Fort d'Espagne (Spanish Fort) testify to its pirate past when the corsairs would speed home and frustrate pursuers by hiding behind strong walls and Turkish cannons. The octagonal minaret of the Grand Mosque is another reminder of the coast's Turkish past. Visits to the mosque can be arranged through the tourist office *(Syndicat d'Initiative)*.

Interested in other sorts of glitter, the pirates ignored the golden stretch of sand which is now Bizerta's greatest treasure. The famous **Corniche**, several miles west of the town, is furnished with good hotels and appreciative tourists who enjoy what the pirates missed.

To the east of Bizerta, GHAR EL MELH is another 17th-century pirate port, complete with several Turkish fortresses and mosques. The drive to the nearby *koubba* (dome) of SIDI ALI EL MEKKI passes alongside a fine beach, and there's yet another beautiful strip of sand at RAF-RAF.

Utica *(Utique)*

Tunisia's history starts with the Phoenicians, and their first important settlement was established here at Utica in about 1,100 B.C. The sea, which once came right to Utica's doorstep, later receded and took with it the town's importance. A small museum preserves the relics found in Punic tombs, and some interesting vestiges of Roman patricians' houses near the museum inspire visions of Utica in its heyday.

The Coral Coast

West of Bizerta the coast is wild, untouched, private and beautiful. The roads to CAP SERRAT are not very good, but the swimming, fishing and coral-diving are excellent. Back on the Bizerta-Tabarka highway, the town of SEDJENANE provides contrast: mining is the main industry here, and local potters produce curious little statuettes. Making any sort of image is against the tenets of Islam, but these craftsmen and women refuse to be parted from a pagan Berber tradition over a thousand years old.

Back on the coast at SIDI MECHRIG, the pace of life is slow. Fishing and bringing up coral twigs occupies the villagers almost completely, but the few adventurous tourists who wander into town usually find the beach pretty absorbing, too. A little farther along the coast, CAP NEGRO has allure for the same reasons with the added bonus of a fine view for those who don't mind a short climb. TABARKA, a sleepy town for eight months of the year, comes to life in July and August with its "We're here for more than the sun!" festival. Apart from these lively few weeks, Tabarka's main attraction is coral.

Uncompromising sea-lovers will want to know about the islands of LA GALITE, 24 miles off-shore. No regular boat service connects the few islands to the mainland, no luxury hotels await the sun-seeker. Few people live here, and those who do spend almost all their time fishing with line, net and snorkel for lobster, octopus, mullet, squid, tunny and many other varieties of marine life.

Before heading back to more populous parts of the country, take a detour about 24 km. (15 miles) south for a look at the quaint forest town of AÏN DRAHAM, where the white houses have peaked red tile roofs, and the surrounding hills are covered in cork trees. Even farther south, the ruins of the Roman city of BULLA REGIA are ancient and impressive.

What to Do

Sports

With over 600 miles of coastline and numerous islands, Tunisia is like a dream come true for all who love the sea. Good swimming along perfect white sand beaches is right at the doorstep of any resort hotel. If the weather is a bit chilly, opt for the hotel's heated pool—most places have at least one, and some give you a choice of fresh or salt water. Hotels also rent out sailboats and rowing-boats. In a few places, water skiing is available.

Fishermen can cast line or net anywhere and even arrange to go out with a commercial fishing boat on a daily run. Have the proper gear, as your hook may be swallowed by anything from a sardine to a tunny. Underwater fishing is popular and has the added advantage of being productive of delicious dinners: mullet, grouper, shrimp or lobster can be a skilful diver's main course.

Nets ready on deck, these fishermen chug away from Bizerta's vieux port, once a pirates' lair.

Cap Bon is a favourite area for undersea fishing, especially at Kélibia and Sidi Daoud. From Sidi Daoud, boats take amateur divers out to the Isle of Zembra, centre for sailing, diving and other water sports. The Iles de Kerkenna (Kerkenna Islands), just off the coast near Sfax, and Adjim on the island of Djerba are the best places for sponge diving.

For underwater fishing, you'll have to pick up a permit from the Ministry of Agriculture and Fisheries, a simple matter. The Centre Nautique International de Tunisie (CNIT), 6, Place de la Monnaie, Tunis, can give you full information on all water sports.

Tennis, Ping-pong, Volleyball Many resorts have their own tennis courts and ping-pong tables for guests, and a few are even lit for night-time play. Don't be disappointed if you've brought your racket and tennis whites only to find that your hotel has no courts. A nearby hotel is sure to have them and will welcome you and your backhand for a nominal fee. Chances are that guests at that same hotel will be wandering over to your domain to use the volleyball court—the spirit is very much share-and-share-alike.

Desert safaris provide plenty of spectacular scenery and unforgettable moments; cooler alternatives abound on Tunisia's Mediterranean coasts.

Desert Safaris

Any travel agent in Tunisia will be glad to tell you about organized treks into the Sahara by Land-Rover. Challenging the elements brings its rewards: after you've pitched your tent, Bedouin-like, at an oasis, the cool evening air and shower of stars are yours to enjoy. A campfire brings everyone close, throwing shadows against the umbrella of palms. By day the desert is another world, beautifully seductive in its shapes, overwhelming in its vastness, deadly to the imprudent. A trip into the desert is something that you're likely to remember for the rest of your life.

Riding

Most of your riding will be on trusty bicycles or the two-seater "surreys" rented from your hotel, but don't miss the chance for a trail ride on horseback, especially if you visit Djerba. Sign up in advance at a hotel with a stable so you're not disappointed.

Final graduation in Tunisian riding circles is to camelback. The huge beasts with the all-too-spindly legs are sure to be brought round for the curi-

ous and intrepid. Go on, try it! The camel (actually it's a dromedary) sits while you mount, the ride will be a short one (there's more camera-snapping than trotting), and the folks back home won't believe their eyes when they see the photographs.

Hunting and Bird Watching

Duck shooting is good at Tunisia's lakes and marshes: woodcock and quail can be found in Khroumirie. The big-   **81** gest excitement comes on a hunt for wild boar on Cap Bon, but for more relaxed shooting try clay pigeons at the Club de Chasse near Tunis. Permits from the Ministère de l'Agriculture are required to import your rifle and ammunition, and to hunt.

If hunting with rifles isn't your cup of tea, try using binoculars. People are not the only escapees to Tunisia from the cold European winter. Most of the continent's migratory birds either spend the winter in Tunisia or fly over it to even warmer places. Over 400 species have been sighted, everything from the egret to the quick-moving pratincole.

Golf

Have you ever made a drive into the spicy eucalyptus, or had your ball bring down an orange? When you golf in Tunisia, even going into the rough can be a pleasure. You can bring your clubs, or hire bag, clubs, balls and shoes at the Golf Club Country [sic] of Carthage, about 7 miles from Tunis at La Soukra. A comfortable terrace, dining room and bar make up the 19th hole.

A new championship golf course at Port El Kantaoui near Sousse also offers all modern facilities.

Folklore

A Tunisian street scene is an exotic sight. Many elements combine to make it that way: the white houses with blue trim, the call to prayer from the minaret, and the unfamiliar Tunisian costumes. Though many city-dwellers dress in modern style, you are more likely to see men in *jellabas*, the light cotton or wool shirts dropping almost to the ankles. In cooler weather the *jellabas* will be covered by a thick hooded woollen burnous to serve as raincoat, overcoat and even sleeping bag. Though a few older men in the professions will keep sun and rain off their heads with a tasselled red *tarboosh* (fez), most others wear the simple red felt *chechia* (skull-cap). To add panache, a scarf may be wound around either hat.

Women's costumes are much more elaborate, and a bride all turned out on her wedding day is a magnificent sight. From the everyday shroud (*safserie*) and veil (*haïk*), the girl is transformed into a dazzling beauty covered with variegated

Once in a lifetime: a bride's trousseau turns her into a princess for that all-important day.

silks and cloths of gold and silver, all set off by a veritable king's ransom in jewellery: rings and bangles, earrings, head-dresses, necklaces, brooches, belts and sashes.

Traditional weddings are held after harvest time and may take as long as a week. Processions of merry-makers—these days often in cars—wind through the town and bags of crimson henna are brought from the perfumer's and used to decorate the bride's hands.

Festivals

Many festivals are determined by the feast days of the Moslem calendar, based on lunar months (see p. 120). The lunar year is 11 days shorter than the solar year, and so the dates of religious holidays are that many days earlier each year.

During the holy month of **Ramadan,** there's fasting during daylight hours, feasting at night. On **Mouled** (Mohammed's birthday) special prayers and ceremonies take place in mosques. The two *Aïds* (celebrations), known as the **Aïd el-Séghir** (or **Aïd el-Fitr**) and the **Aïd el-Kébir** (or **Aïd el-Idha**), come after the Holy month. They commemorate, among other things,

Abraham's near-sacrifice of his son, with many families sacrificing sheep. The other major religious holiday in Tunisia, the Moslem New Year, **Ras el âm el Hejri,** is celebrated with much feasting and well-wishing.

Other festivals during the year include:

Regional Music and Folklore Festivals (April and May). Held in many cities, including Gabès, Gafsa, Kairouan, Monastir, Nefta, Sbeïtla, Sousse and Tabarka (see p. 77).

Festival International de Carthage (Carthage International Festival—July and August). Music, dance and dramatic performances in the

Centre Culturel International.

Festival d'Ulysse (Ulysses Festival—July and early August). Djerba. Folklore, artistic presentations and parades.

Festival d'Eté (Summer Festival—last week in July). Nabeul. Fair, processions, music and a carnival atmosphere.

Festival du Sahara (Festival of the Sahara—December). Douz. Shooting competitions, ceremonies, camel fights and *fantasias* (see p. 69).

Museums

Each important town has its museum of folklore and popular arts, and in Tunis the stupendous collections of the Bardo (see p. 37) are yours to enjoy.

The entry charges to most museums are minimal. Opening hours: from 9.30 a.m.– 4.30 p.m., closed Mondays, but it's always best to check beforehand, as slight variations do sometimes occur.

Tunisia's museums are rich in precious mosaics and fine statuary. Roman artists depicted the bounty of the country's land and seas, as can be seen in these colourful fishing scenes in the Bardo, Tunis.

Sheep abound in Moslem Tunisia, and beautiful wool carpets are a natural by-product. Years of experience yields high-quality work.

Shopping

The crowded *souks* of any Tunisian town are a scene straight from the *Arabian Nights.* Whether it's a small, inexpensive leather coin purse or a huge carpet worth a fortune, something is sure to draw your attention—and capture a portion of your savings. Shops in the *souks* usually stay open from early morning to early evening. Even on Sundays, when most businesses are closed, a few independent-minded shopkeepers remain open all day.

You will see just how alive tradition and local colour have remained; in a noisy, bustling, cheerful atmosphere you will

wander round, picking out whatever catches your eye, haggling, gesticulating, chatting like mad—as best you can.

Whether you decide to buy from the local sellers or the Office National de l'Artisanat (O.N.A.), multilingual, helpful and very persuasive salesmen will offer a broad, interesting selection of the best regional products. To bargain well, you have to stay firm, know your mind... and keep smiling; a compromise price

can usually be found, providing you are patient and not aggressive.

Best Buys
Nothing will be a better souvenir of your Tunisian adventure than a rich hand-woven **carpet** of creamy-soft wool. Actually, Tunisian carpets are of three different kinds. The knotted carpets with a thick pile in traditional or modern designs are found every-

where. *Klims* are mats woven without a pile in designs tending to the geometric. *Mergoums* are a bit of both: mats of a plain, solid-colour warp and embroidered with bright, intricate geometric patterns during the weaving. Kairouan is especially famous for its carpets called *zerbia*, inspired by Anatolian Turkish pieces.

Shopkeepers in Kairouan and most other towns offer to take visitors to see the weavers at work. Seeing the labour and skill that goes into the making of any carpet will help you to understand the prices for these masterpieces of craftsmanship. At Artisanats, all carpets are classed and labelled. Prices are based on the density of knots and may range from 20 to 200 Dinars per square metre of carpet. *Klims* and *mergoums* cost about 16 to 20 Dinars per square metre. Artisanat shops will wrap and ship your purchase (at an extra charge) if you buy at least 50 Dinars' worth of goods.

If a carpet is too expensive, Tunisian **wool blankets** are almost as nice and considerably cheaper. They even come with stylized figures and geometric patterns. Colours in beige to brown mean all-wool blankets, while bright colours are a sign of synthetic fabrics and dyes.

In Hammamet and Nabeul, **embroidery** is a speciality whether it embellishes a tablecloth or an evening gown. Wearable souvenirs are everywhere: inexpensive shirts with gaily coloured embroidery, cotton, wool or silk caftans blazing with gold thread (they make striking hostess gowns), even tent-like burnouses are on sale.

Leather goods of all types are piled high in every shop, including every possible contrivance to carry money: coin purses, wallets and ladies' handbags abound, as do satchels and suitcases. Prices and quality vary, so it's advisable to shop around.

Vessels in copper, brass and pottery are inexpensive, attractive and make good conversation pieces.

Antiques

The most sought-after antiques are authentic Berber jewellery and artefacts from Tunisia's Punic and Roman past. The fakes outnumber the genuine articles by at least a hundred to one. Don't pay for a "collector's

Haggling is a social custom that both sides can enjoy. Results are low prices—and new friends.

88

item" unless you are a collector and are sure of its value. Often the modern copies are interesting and attractive pieces in their own right, and well worth having, but not at "antique" prices.

Souvenirs

Though miniature camel saddles, knick-knacks portraying Berber women, and plastic palm trees have begun to appear, most Tunisian souvenirs are eminently useful. Coasters and ashtrays of pounded copper, small squares of carpet for use as seat-mats or a painted coffee mug will serve as an inexpensive and easily portable reminder of your trip. Silver jewellery is attractive and not overly expensive, and though most is designed for women, a few things, such as rings and belt buckles, are made for men as well.

Bargaining

Bargaining in the *souks* is more than a means of determining price. It's a time-honoured social ritual as well. In an economy where products are hand-made, each one unique, bargaining helps both buyer and seller to decide prices. To get the best price one must know the market by browsing

in several shops and asking the prices of comparable pieces. But an easier and less time-consuming way—and guaranteed to avoid dissatisfaction—is simply to find something you like and decide what it's worth to you. For instance, if an attractive wallet or purse looks well-made and would cost the equivalent of 5 Dinars at home, you might decide it's worth 4 Dinars to you here. Ask the price: if the shopkeeper says "three", you have a bargain; if he says "five", offer him four, and he will usually accept. There is no shame in walking away after you've bargained, except that you really should buy if the seller meets your price.

If all this is too oriental for your taste, remember that the Artisanat shops all have fixed prices guaranteed to be moderate.

Nightlife

The Tunisian coast comes alive at night. It's almost as though the radiant energy absorbed during the day has been stored up to be worked off at night. Many resort hotels have their own discotheques, bars and nightclubs, and the practice of hotel-hopping allows easy access to the crowds and combos of other hostelries in your area. Most hotels sponsor an evening of folk dancing and Tunisian music at least once a week, and many also arrange tours to little night-spots (boîtes) in the médinas of nearby towns. Nurseries at the larger hotels will keep the children happy.

During the months of high summer, festivals organized for one reason or another animate most coastal towns and villages in the evening. During the holy month of Ramadan, when all food and drink is prohibited to good Moslems during daylight hours, the evening is a time for feasting and merrymaking, and the infectious fun-loving spirit spreads to tourists and Tunisians alike.

Special Places

Each resort has its particular attractions. In Tunis over a dozen cinemas show films in Arabic and French. The Maison de la Culture (cultural centre) "Ibn Khaldun" usually has an entertaining film running and often an exhibition of paintings, drawings or photographs as well. Concerts of symphony and chamber music as well as Tunisian folk music take place all year and particularly in the autumn, winter and spring. Tours by internationally known concert and popular music stars add to evening attractions, and the occasional performance of a malouf, the strange, traditional Tunisian musical cycle brought centuries ago from Spain by Moorish immigrants, is a special treat.

Cinemas and symphony concerts are big-city entertainments, and they are not too easily found outside of Tunis and Sousse, though some large resort hotels sponsor their own cinema evenings. In smaller towns, other shows easily fill the gap. Hammamet has its Centre Culturel International, where frequent dramatic and musical events are staged in the opulent grounds of a luxurious former private estate. For contrast, traditional Tunisian entertainments delight spectators in the romantic setting of Hammamet's medieval kasba. The forbidding ribats of Sousse and Monastir are fitted out in summer with benches for visitors who have come to relive the gallant days of Moslem chivalry through a sound-and-light show. In Djerba the hotels have their own high-decibel, high-excitement clubs. The town of Houmt Souk has quaint boîtes and congenial outdoor cafés for a change of scene. **91**

Wining and Dining

Imagine all the men who have ruled Tunisia over the centuries sitting together in a restaurant and ordering their favourite dishes. Arabic *couscous* or *tajine*, liberally spiced with fiery *harissa* peppers. Turkish *chorba*, *brik* and *doulma*, and finely prepared dishes from the French tradition would all grace the table. Today, the national cuisine of Tunisia bears a strong resemblance to such a banquet.

Appetizers

A tangy plate of *méchouia* is a good introduction to the staples: olive oil, tomatoes, hot peppers, onions, salted lemons and capers are cooked together and sprinkled with chunks of tunny fish and hard-boiled eggs. Another favourite first course is crusty *brik*, a thin pastry envelope filled with egg, cheese or meat, sealed and fried in olive oil. Romantic-sounding *doigts de Fatima* (Fatima's

No need to wait until after dinner for this favourite sweet: market-stalls sell maqroudh all day long.

92

fingers) are a sausage-shaped variation of *brik*. If you've never tried brains, you may get your chance if *odjja* is offered. Little balls of meat, fish, or brains mixed with salt, pepper, mint and coriander are cooked up in a sauce of tomatoes, hot peppers, eggs, garlic and caraway to make a flavoursome stew. If you shy away from spicy food, try a bowl of savoury lamb vermicelli soup called *chorba*, which in theory is not too hot.

Seafood

The selection of seafood dishes is limited only by the Mediterranean itself, and in coastal towns the dorado, mullet, perch, mackerel and halibut are sure to be fresh and tasty. Don't miss stuffed fish if you come across it. A common stuffing uses eggs, olive oil, cheese, parsley and onion. Besides fish, menus offer shrimp, squid and octopus, and—if you're very lucky and ahead of your budget—lobster.

Main Courses

Every Tunisian housewife learns while she is a girl to make perfect grains of *couscous* in at least three different sizes. Though restaurants obtain their supplies of this semolina staple from the market, the cooked-up results are equally delicious. A special earthenware *couscousier* is used to cook the semolina and to prepare meat, chick-peas and vegetables. Served in its own particular dish on a little pedestal, the *couscous* comes moistened with broth and topped with meat and vegetables, and takes top honours as the national dish.

Marrow (squash) or green peppers stuffed with meat, parsley, onion and eggs makes another good hot main course called *doulma*.

Tajines are vegetable-and-egg stews cooked in an earthenware casserole and are often based on spinach or cheese.

Cheese

Traditional recipes use a number of cheeses such as *mateur*, a fresh white cheese, and others made from ewe's milk and goat's milk. The French, luckily for visitors today, introduced a blue cheese called *numidia*, similar to Roquefort.

Desserts and Sweetmeats

No after dinner treat can compare with a pair of juicy *clémentines* (tangerines, mandarin oranges), but if these are not in season, perhaps there will be *degla mehcheya* (dates stuffed with almonds, sugar and rose water). *Assida*, a sweet custard made with hazel-nuts and milk and eggs, is decorated with pistachios, crushed hazel and pine nuts for a special treat on festive occasions. Fancier restaurants often have good selections of *gâteaux* and pastries for those who have exercised enough to ignore dieting.

Snacks

The town market is a fine place to pick up a snack. Any fruit stall will hold a half-dozen of the season's best offerings, and a man with a portable glass box will sell you *maqroudh* (sweet semolina cakes with date stuffing) for a few Millimes apiece. More elaborate glass boxes on wheels are actually peripatetic sandwich shops, and for 200 Millimes or thereabouts the "chef" will stuff a roll with cheese, tunny, tomato, onion and the ever-present (but easily removable) hot pepper. The sandwiches are called *casse-croûte*.

Coffee and Cafés

It is said that an Arab goatherd discovered coffee when he found his goats eating the berries and gambolling about with more than usual energy. The discovery of the stimulating brew changed life throughout the world, not least in Tunisia. No matter how sleepy and rest-ful a café may be by day, it is a Tunisian's favourite resort in the evening. Tables are crowded, conversation is spirited, sometimes even drowning out the noise from the ever-present television set. Besides coffee, you can order mint tea, soft drinks, snacks, sandwiches and sometimes even beer, wine and liqueurs. If you have the time, try out a few different cafés to see which suits you best.

Wine and Spirits

The Phoenicians planted vineyards soon after arriving in Tunisia, and so the country can boast more than two thousand years of winemaking. The Romans increased and refined the art, but the coming of the Moslem teetotalers forced most vineyards to sell their wares as fruit rather than wine. Under the Protectorate the industry revived and modernized until today it boasts equipment and methods as up-to-date as anywhere in the world. Several dozen labels may come your way. Among the reds, *Coteaux de Carthage* and *Haut Mornag* are especially favoured, while a leader among the whites is *Sidi Rais*. Unique among sweet wines is the "dry-sweet" *Muscat Sec de Kélibia*, with a special quality found nowhere else. **95**

Many French aperitifs and liqueurs appear on the shelves of cafés and bars in Tunisia, but these drinks, along with such exotic imports as whisky and foreign beer, are more expensive than local products. To save money, try *Thibarine*, the Tunisian date liqueur similar in taste to *Cointreau*. Adventurous drinkers can order a small bottle (8.75 centilitres) of a dry fig brandy called *boukha*. The flavour is only vaguely reminiscent of figs, while the effect on the throat is distinctly one of liquid razor blades.

The most popular Tunisian beer is a palatable light lager named *Celtia*. Other local beers and several imported ones as well, fill café coolers from Tunis to the desert oases.

Mineral Water

Though the carafe of tap water on your table is pure and potable, bottled mineral water is always safer and more salubrious. *Safia* and *Melliti* are the most widely available still waters, *faiblement minéralisées* (with a light concentration of minerals). *Aïn Garci* and *Aïn Oktor* are similar but fizzy. Convenient quarter-litre bottles are not found everywhere, but the litre size does well for two at dinner.

Mint Tea—A Ceremony

No visit to a Tunisian home could be complete without the friendly hocus-pocus of mint tea. A squat and curvy pot of silver, pewter, aluminium or enamel is filled with boiling water, then emptied. Next, large quantities of sugar and green tea are jammed into the pot together with cold water which is then boiled. When ready, more water and sugar, and now also mint, are added according to taste.

The mixture is poured into a glass, then back into the pot and finally—the supreme moment—the tea is streamed back into the glasses from the pot high above. (Needless to say, the host's good aim with the boiling liquid is crucial to the success of the ceremony.) After each round the pot is topped up with water and, in theory, children and elderly people are only served the weaker, third round.

Though you may not have the chance to visit a Tunisian home, you can still enjoy the tea in any café, without, alas, the touch of the traditional ceremony.

In a silver service or straight from the pot, all Tunisians enjoy mint tea, strong and sweet.

To Help You Order...

Do you have a table?
Do you have a set-price menu?
I'd like a/an/some...

Avez-vous une table?
Avez-vous un menu à prix fixe?
J'aimerais...

beer	une bière	pepper	du poivre
bread	du pain	potatoes	pommes de terre
coffee	un café		
dessert	du dessert	rice	du riz
fish	du poisson	salad	de la salade
fork	une fourchette	salt	du sel
fruit	un fruit	sandwich	un sandwich
glass	un verre	soup	de la soupe
ice-cream	une glace	spoon	une cuiller
knife	un couteau	sugar	du sucre
meat	de la viande	tea (mint)	un thé (à la menthe)
menu	la carte		
milk	du lait	water (iced)	de l'eau (glacée)
mineral water	de l'eau minérale	wine	du vin

98

...and Read the Menu

agneau	lamb	**escargots**	snails
ail	garlic	**figues**	figs
ananas	pineapple	**foie**	liver
artichaut	artichoke	**fraises**	strawberries
anchois	anchovies	**framboises**	raspberries
asperges	asparagus	**fromage (de**	cheese (goat's)
aubergine	aubergine, eggplant	**chèvre)**	
		gâteau	cake
banane	banana	**homard**	lobster
beurre	butter	**huile**	oil
biftek	beefsteak	**huîtres**	oysters
bœuf	beef	**langouste**	spiny lobster
boulettes	meatballs	**légumes**	vegetables
brochette	skewered meat or fish	**merguez**	spicy sausage
		moules	mussels
calmar	squid	**moutarde**	mustard
carottes	carrots	**mouton**	mutton
champignons	mushrooms	**noix**	nuts
chorba	soup	**nouilles**	noodles
chou	cabbage	**œufs**	eggs
chou-fleur	cauliflower	**oignons**	onions
citron	lemon	**pamplemousse**	grapefruit
clémentine	tangerine	**pêche**	peach
concombre	cucumber	**persil**	parsley
confiture	jam	**poire**	pear
côtelettes d'agneau	lamb chops	**pois chiches**	chick-peas
		pomme	apple
courge, cour- gette	marrow, zuc- chini (squash)	**poulet**	chicken
		poulpe	octopus
couscous	steamed semolina	**raisins**	grapes
		rognons	kidneys
crevettes	shrimp	**saucisse**	sausage
dattes	dates	**saumon**	salmon
daurade	dorado, sea bream	**tarte**	tart, pie
		thon	tunny, tuna fish
entrecôte	rib eye steak	**tomate**	tomato
épinards	spinach	**veau**	veal
		viande	meat

99

How to Get There

From Great Britain

BY AIR: Direct, non-stop scheduled flights leave from London to Tunis four times weekly. There are special reductions for students, husband and wife, children and for mid-week travel.

For the best bargains sign up on a package tour which includes flight, hotel and meals. Although you travel with a group you're free to do as you please once you reach your destination. Since many travel agencies offer tours to different Tunisian resorts you should compare prices and services offered.

BY SEA: Several companies operate car and passenger ferries between European ports and Tunis. Services are more frequent (and the fares higher) in summer. From Genoa, Italy, you can get an overnight connection on large, comfortable ferries; these same companies also take on passengers at Naples, Palermo and Cagliari. From France both Tunisian and French lines operate to Tunis from Marseilles.

From North America

BY AIR: There are direct flights from a dozen American cities and from Montreal and Toronto in Canada to European destinations (such as Paris or Frankfurt) from where there are daily connections to Tunis, Monastir–Skanès and Djerba. Non-stop flights leave from Zurich to Djerba, so if that southern isle is your final destination, you might like to fly via Zurich rather than from another city which might require you to change planes at Tunis. Other major cities with daily flights to Tunis are Rome, Paris and Frankfurt (except Tuesdays).

Regular excursion and APEX (Advance Purchase Excursion) fares are money-savers. Since regulations change constantly, before you leave you should always check with a reliable travel agent for the latest information on fares.

Low season rates are in effect from September 1 to May 31. Youth fares are offered for those between 12 and 21; you confirm upon booking and the ticket is valid for one year.

Various package tours are offered from North America to Tunisia as well as to other points in North Africa and Europe. Tunisian tours usually run for two weeks or longer and feature such diverse activities as touring the desert by jeep or visiting art treasures.

From Australia and New Zealand

Flights leave Melbourne for Frankfurt from where direct flights for Tunis leave every day of the week except Tuesdays.

From Auckland visitors have the choice of travelling via Bombay and Cairo to Tunis, or a European destination from where there are daily flights.

From North Africa

Frequent flights and daily train services connect Tunis with Algiers. A new airport, a mile or two from Tozeur, now serves southern Tunisia.

From Algiers and Tripoli owners of estate (station) wagons operate services *(voitures de louage)* to Tunis every day. There are two main garages in Tunis (one on Farhet Hached, the other at Place Sidi Bayan). Savings over air fare is considerable and such a trip is indisputably an adventure!

When to Go

The beaches in Tunisia are best for sunbathing from late April to late October. Outside of these months some chilly days drive swimmers to the heated hotel pools. From late November to March, the emphasis is on relaxation, cultural offerings and excursions into the desert. In winter the temperature in the desert or on Djerba can be a cool 16 °C (60 °F) during the day. In contrast, summer temperatures can rise to 40 °C (100 °F).

Whether you go in winter, spring, summer or autumn, the difference between the daily high and low temperatures can be as much as 10–15 °C (20–30 °F), and so you'll want a pullover or light jacket on summer evenings, and something warmer for the winter. There's not much rain in summer, and even in spring and autumn rainfall is relatively sparse; in winter, however, it's essential to have a raincoat with you.

Off-season tours may save a good deal of money, but be prepared for a cloudy day or two, no matter what the brochures may say. Much depends on the year: some winters are very mild indeed, and off-season visitors get the best weather of all. Other times a holiday week may pass cool and overcast—but even so, certainly warmer than at home.

The following charts will give you an idea of the monthly average temperatures in Tunis and Djerba and the average water temperature at Tunisian beaches:

		J	F	M	A	M	J	J	A	S	O	N	D
Air temperature													
Tunis	°C	11	12	13	16	19	24	26	26	26	20	16	12
	°F	52	54	55	61	66	75	79	79	79	68	61	54
Djerba	°C	11	13	16	19	21	24	27	28	26	23	16	14
	°F	52	55	61	66	69	75	81	82	79	72	61	57
Water temperature													
	°C	14	13	14	16	18	21	24	26	26	24	17	11
	°F	57	55	57	61	64	69	75	79	79	75	63	52

Planning Your Budget

To give you an idea of what to expect, here are some average prices in Tunisian Dinars. However, take into account that all prices must be regarded as approximate.

Baby-sitters. 700 M to 1 D an hour.

Bicycle hire. 500 M to 1 D per hour.

Camping. 600 M per person (children half price), tent/caravan (trailer)/car 800 M each per day.

Car hire. *Fiat 127* 8.5 D per day, 80 M per km., 150 D per week with unlimited mileage. *Fiat 131/Renault 18* 14 D per day, 100 M per km., 280 D per week with unlimited mileage (when available). Add 7.5% tax.

Cigarettes. Tunisian 170–360 M per packet of 20, foreign brands 620 M to 1 D.

Cinema. 300 M to 1 D.

Discotheque (admission and first drink). 1.5–2.5 D.

Guides and interpreters. *Guides* half-day 5–7 D, full day 8–10 D. *Interpreters* 5 D an hour.

Hairdressers. Haircut 1–4 D, shampoo and set 2.5 D. Tip 15–20%.

Hotels (double room with bath). ****L 18–25 D, **** 11–18 D, *** 6–14 D, ** 4–10 D, * 3–8 D, no stars 4–6 D.

Meals and drinks. Continental breakfast 700 M to 1.6 D, three-course meal 2–7 D, espresso coffee 100–300 M, aperitif (French) 700 M to 1.2 D, beer 300–500 M, soft drinks 150–300 M.

Shopping bag. Bread (½ kilo) 50 M, butter (¼ kilo) 300 M, cheese (½ kilo) 500 M to 2 D, potatoes (1 kilo) 200 M, beefsteak (1 kilo) 2.1 D, coffee (¼ kilo) 1.1 D, milk (1 litre) 200 M, wine (1 litre) 560 M to 1.2 D, beer (small bottle) 200 M.

Taxi (mini). Meter charge around 160 M, plus 120 M per kilometre.

Youth hostels. 500 M to 1 D per night, 250 M for breakfast, 800 M to 1 D for lunch or dinner.

BLUEPRINT for a Perfect Trip

An A-Z Summary of Practical Information and Facts

Listed after most main entries is an equivalent French expression, usually in the singular.

The information in this section has been carefully checked prior to publication. However, changes are bound to occur and we should be pleased to hear from readers of any new developments. For prices, refer to list on page 103.

Contents

Airports
Alphabet
Bus Services
Camping
Car Hire
Children (baby-sitting, nurseries, etc.)
Cigarettes, Cigars, Tobacco
Clothing
Communications (post-office hours, mail, telegrams, telephone)
Complaints
Consulates and Embassies
Converter Charts
Driving in Tunisia
Electric Current
Emergencies
Entry Formalities and Customs Controls
Guides and Interpreters
Haggling
Hitch-hiking
Hotels and Accommodation
Language

Laundry and Dry-cleaning
Lost Property
Louages
Maps
Medical Care
Meeting People
Money matters (currency, banking hours, traveller's cheques, credit cards)
Newspapers and Magazines
Photography
Police
Public Holidays
Radio and TV
Religious Services
Siesta
Taxi
Time Differences
Tipping
Toilets
Tourist Information Offices
Trains
Water
Youth Hostels
Some Useful Expressions

CONTENTS

104

AIRPORTS *(aéroport).* The international airport of Tunis-Carthage is 8 kilometres from the centre of Tunis. It's a modern, well-organized complex with all the services you'll need, including a duty-free shop, currency exchange facilities, travel agencies, car hire desks, a restaurant and a coffee bar. Porters are available, but most passengers will find it more convenient to use the free luggage trolleys. Municipal bus No. 35 runs from the airport to the T.G.M. terminal on Place d'Afrique in Tunis every 30 minutes, and tickets cost a fraction of the mini-taxi fare.

The international airports at Skanès–Monastir (8 km. from Monastir) and Mellita on the island of Djerba (6 km. from Houmt Souk) are also modern with a full range of services. Buses and *louages* (shared taxis; see separate entry) serve both airports.

In 1978, a new airport 3 kilometres from Tozeur was opened to serve the Tunisian south.

Where's the bus for …?   **D'où part le bus pour …?**

ALPHABET. See also LANGUAGE. The Arabic alphabet is a beautiful and expressive means of writing, but it's also difficult to learn. The 28 characters of the alphabet have different shapes, depending on whether they appear at the beginning, in the middle, or at the end of a word. In addition, the various different scripts change and stylize the letters, sometimes making them even harder to recognize, and normally only the consonants are written. The vowels (little marks and squiggles above and below the line of writing) appear only in the Koran and in learners' books. If the beginner can master all these difficulties, the fact that Arabic is written from right to left will prove no problem!

Fortunately, every major public sign in Tunisia is in both Arabic and French, as are timetables, menus and official notices. By equipping yourself with a modicum of French you should be able to manage.

BUS SERVICES *(autobus).* Tunis has a very convenient network of city buses. Maps of the system are posted in the terminals. Other cities have good public transport facilities as well; even on Djerba, buses connect Houmt Souk with the airport, hotel zone and other towns and villages.

Inter-city buses are another matter. Regional bus systems provide adequate service within a given *gouvernorat* (county), but the national network should only be tried by the travel-hardened and very patient. For long-distance travel by road, you're better off going by shared taxi (see LOUAGES).

B   When's the next bus to…?   **Quand part le prochain bus**
                                       pour…?

single (one-way)   **aller simple**
return (round-trip)   **aller et retour**

C   **CAMPING** *(camping)*. Camping sites with electricity, water and shops
are only now making an appearance in Tunisia, but that should not stop
you from packing your tent or trailing your caravan south for a few
weeks. Simple camping grounds have been established near Ham-
mam-Lif, Hammamet, Gabès, Nabeul and Zarzis (for prices, see p.
103). In other places you are free to set up camp wherever you like, but
use discretion and good sense. If it's clear who the owner of the land is,
ask permission. The National Tourist Office can provide current prices
and information about the recognized camping sites.

May we camp here?   **Pouvons-nous camper ici, s'il vous**
                                       plaît?

CAR HIRE *(location de voitures)*. Several large international firms and
also a number of small local agencies rent cars. Prices vary greatly
depending on the size and comfort of the car. Availability can be a
problem, particularly with the less expensive, more popular models, so
it's a good idea to reserve a car in advance (which is usually easier to do
through a car hire firm in your own country).

   To hire a car you'll need a valid national driving licence held for at
least a year, and you must be over 21 years old. A deposit will be required unless you have an approved credit card (see also p. 103). Third-
party, fire and theft insurance is included, but you have to pay extra for
personal injury and collision coverage. A tax of 7.5 per cent will be
added to the total of the rental, except on the registration tax charged
for each contract and the petrol necessary to fill the tank upon return of
the car. See also DRIVING.

I'd like to hire a car (tomorrow).   **Je voudrais louer une voiture**
                                       (demain).

for one day/a week   **pour une journée/une semaine**
Please include full insurance.   **Avec assurance tous risques, s'il**
                                       vous plaît.

CHILDREN. The large resort hotels provide baby-sitting services and
many also staff a nursery as a free service to guests. Some even run
special children's programmes of entertainment and games throughout

the week. For baby-sitting, tell the *concierge* well in advance so he can make arrangements.

Children who wander off tend to be located soon after, looking bewildered in the company of an equally bewildered Tunisian. Often this drama ends in a café, shop or hotel restaurant. The best thing you can do is let as many people as possible know you're looking for a lost child, and soon you'll have cast a wide net almost certain to get results. If all else fails, contact the local police or the Garde Nationale.

Can you get me a baby-sitter for tonight?	**Pouvez-vous me trouver une garde d'enfants pour ce soir?**
I'm looking for my child.	**Je cherche mon enfant.**

CIGARETTES, CIGARS, TOBACCO (*cigarettes, cigares, tabac*). Because of tourist demand, many brands of foreign cigarettes are sold by Tunisian tobacconists (*tabac;* in Arabic, دخان*—duhan*). However, except for popular French brands, it's difficult to find imported cigarettes outside resort areas or big cities.

Tunisian cigarettes are manufactured by a government monopoly, and have less flavour than foreign brands. If you'd like to try a Tunisian brand but you don't want to risk buying a whole packet, look for street vendors, many of whom sell single cigarettes to those low on capital. For prices, see page 103.

A few of the more popular brands of cigars are also sold by street vendors, but in general cigars are not easy to come by. Pipe tobacco is rarely found outside the big hotels; best bring a supply of your own (see ENTRY FORMALITIES AND CUSTOMS CONTROLS).

A packet of…/A box of matches, please.	**Un paquet de…/Une boîte d'allumettes, s'il vous plaît.**
filter-tipped/without filter	**avec/sans filtre**
light/dark tobacco	**du tabac blond/brun**

CLOTHING. It's always sensible to have a pullover or light jacket, even in summer, as night breezes can be chilly, especially in the desert. In spring, autumn and winter, bring a raincoat and in winter, adequate warm clothing. January temperatures in Tunis can be as low as 7°C.

Though society in Tunis tends to jacket-and-tie formality, the spirit at resort hotels is definitely one of informality. Ladies solve their what-to-wear problem easily and elegantly by buying a caftan—simple, comfortable and acceptable in every conceivable situation. Bathing suits are worn throughout the day at the resort hotels (except in the restaurants), but it's good to change to sports clothes for excursions into the countryside—remember that the local women are veiled.

When visiting mosques, churches and synagogues, proper dress is expected, and on entering a religious sanctuary of any kind, ladies should cover their heads.

COMMUNICATIONS. Post offices *(poste)* are identified by a long rectangular sign with a legend in black Arabic letters on a yellow background. Down in a corner of the sign will be the initials PTT.

Hours

From Sept. 16 to June 30: 8 a.m.–12 noon and 3–6 p.m., Monday to Friday, and 8 a.m.–12 noon on Saturdays.

From July 1 to Sept. 15: 7.30 a.m.–12.30 p.m. and 4.30–6.30 p.m., Monday to Friday.

During the month of Ramadan: 9 a.m.–1.30 p.m., Monday to Saturday.

Though all postal services are available during normal hours, the large post offices maintain longer hours for the sale of stamps and for sending telegrams. In Tunis, Sfax, Houmt Souk and Sousse, these services are available 24 hours a day. Small parcels may be sent from any post office; in Tunis there's a special office for *colis postaux* (parcel post) on Avenue de la République, just off Avenue Habib Bourguiba.

The **main post office** in Tunis is in Rue Charles de Gaulle between Rue d'Espagne and Rue d'Angleterre; the **telegraph office** is in the same building, but the entrance is in Rue Jamel Abdel Nasser. Stamps can also be bought at tobacconists'.

Poste restante (general delivery): If you don't know ahead of time where you'll be staying, you can have your mail addressed poste restante to whichever town is most convenient. You'll have to pay a small charge for each letter received in this way. Take your passport along when you go to collect your mail.

Telephone *(téléphone):* Tunisia's telephone system is operated by the post office and is being converted to nationwide automatic operation which includes the possibility of direct dialling to Europe and soon to North America. For most visitors, however, expensive long-distance calls must be placed through the hotel switchboard or from a post office telephone bureau (usually less expensive than the hotel). It may take 15 minutes to half an hour to get a line, depending on when you call.

In Tunis, the telephone bureau in the main post office (see above) is open 24 hours a day and has a library containing telephone directories covering most of Europe and Africa.

For local calls, *taxiphones* taking 50-Millime coins are available in cafés, hotels, airports and other public places. Unused coins are returned at the end of the call. In principle, *taxiphones* can be used for inter-city and international calls, but in practice one spends more time fumbling with coins than talking.

Can you get me this number in…?	**Pouvez-vous me donner ce numéro à…?**
I want to send a telegram to…	**Je veux envoyer un télégramme à…**
A stamp for this letter/postcard, please.	**Un timbre pour cette lettre/carte postale, s'il vous plaît.**
express (special delivery)	**par exprès**
airmail	**par avion**
registered	**recommandé**
Have you received any mail for…?	**Avez-vous du courrier pour…?**

COMPLAINTS. By far and away the most common complaint in Tunisia comes from tourists who feel they've been overcharged in the *souks* when they see the same or similar items at cheaper prices elsewhere. The best way to avoid this problem is to check prices in one of the numerous state-run Artisanat shops before you buy anything in the *souks.* Then you can make a sensible estimate of the value of items offered for sale (see also p. 90).

There are several ways of lodging an official complaint in Tunisia, but it's rarely necessary to use them. Hotels often have an assistant manager who can help with most problems, and in a restaurant, the maître d'hôtel will usually set things right. Otherwise, each region has its Fédération Régionale des Hôteliers, a hotel-keepers' guild, which will investigate incidents. Hotels, restaurants and licensed guides are required to have complaints books readily available to guests, and you have the right to register any comments, or even to inspect the book before paying for the service. If all else fails, contact the *commissaire de tourisme* (head of the regional tourist office).

CONSULATES and EMBASSIES *(consulat; ambassade)*

Canada: 2, Place Virgile, Notre Dame de Tunis; tel.: (01) 286.577.
Hours: 8 a.m.–5 p.m. on Mondays and Wednesdays,
       8 a.m.–2.30 p.m. on Tuesdays, Thursdays and Fridays.

C **Great Britain:** 5, Place de la Victoire (better known as "Porte de France"), Tunis; tel.: (01) 245.100 (records messages after hours).

Hours: 8 a.m.–1.30 p.m., Monday to Friday.

U.S.A.: 142, Avenue de la Liberté, Tunis; tel.: (01) 282.566.

Hours: 8.30 a.m.–5.30 p.m. in winter, 7.30 a.m.–3.30 p.m. in summer, Monday to Friday all year.

CONVERTER CHARTS. For fluid and distance measures, see pages 111–112. Tunisia uses the metric system.

Temperature

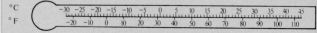

Length

Weight

grams | 0 | 100 | 200 | 300 | 400 | 500 | 600 | 700 | 800 | 900 | 1 kg

ounces | 0 | 4 | 8 | 12 | 1 lb | 20 | 24 | 28 | 2 lb.

D **DRIVING IN TUNISIA**

Entering Tunisia: You may bring your car into the country if you have:

- a national or international driving licence
- car registration papers
- a car insurance policy valid for Tunisia

The insurance is compulsory, and if you don't have a proper international policy that specifies its validity for Tunisia, you'll have to purchase a Tunisian policy at the customs office. Temporary import permits for cars, motorcycles and mopeds are issued free of charge at the frontier for a term of three months and can be renewed for another three months upon payment of certain taxes.

Driving conditions: Rules of the road are the same as those in force in
Europe. Major highways are generally kept in very good condition and

D

there is not a great deal of traffic (at least compared to roads of similar importance in Europe). The speed limit in built-up areas is 40 kilometres an hour, or 25 m.p.h.; on country roads, 100 k.p.h. (62 m.p.h.). Remember that many country people are not good at judging the speed of oncoming cars and if someone is crossing the road or about to cross, slow down to be sure.

Except for a short stretch of motorway (expressway) near Tunis, all roads are for two-way traffic. Heavy vehicles and motorcycles must be overtaken with caution. Be sure to signal each time you turn.

Note: if a map shows a road as paved along its entire length, it is probably good, but any other sort of road should be avoided, no matter how convincingly the map says "good unpaved secondary road". Also, beware of large and impressive directional markers which point the way to "short cut" roads. It's quicker and safer in every case to travel on the roads which are clearly major ones, even if in actual mileage they're a bit longer.

Traffic police: The Garde Nationale patrols major highways to help motorists in distress and chastise lawbreakers. Officers in French-style riding uniforms with jodhpurs use both cars and large motorcycles in their work and it isn't unusual to be stopped for a routine check of car papers. The police are unfailingly courteous if everything is in order. Posts manned by the Garde Nationale are in every town of any size and they should be consulted if you're in any doubt as to road conditions. Desert roads can be covered with sand, other roads can be cut after rainstorms and so it's a good idea to ask often. In fact, it's against the law to venture into the Sahara south of Foum Tataouine without registering your party and itinerary with the Garde Nationale in Médenine.

Fuel and oil: Fuel is sold by the litre, as is oil. Grades are *normale,* also simply called *essence; super* (pronounced "soopair"), or *extra;* and diesel, called *mazout.* Almost every car will run better on super, no matter what you put in at home. Diesel fuel is readily available almost everywhere, as diesel-powered Peugeots are very popular in Tunisia.

Fluid measures

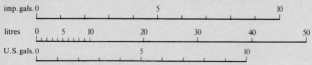

D Distance

Breakdowns and accidents: Most European car manufacturers have representatives in Tunis, and especially for French-made cars spare parts and service are easily found. If there's been an accident and anyone is injured, you are required to contact the Garde Nationale as soon as possible. If the damage is only material, an exchange of pertinent information and insurance policy data is all that's required.

Road signs: Roads are generally well marked and virtually all directional signs are in both French and Arabic. Other signs are the familiar international pictographs. You may encounter these signs as well:

Attention	Caution
Attention travaux	Caution, road works
Crue	Liable to flood during rains
Déviation	Diversion (Detour)
Serrez à droite	Keep to the right
Défense de stationner	No parking
Virages	Bends (Curves)

(international) driving licence	**permis de conduire (international)**
car registration papers	**carte grise**
insurance certificate	**certificat d'assurance**
Are we on the road to…?	**Sommes-nous sur la route de…?**
Fill the tank, please.	**Le plein, s'il vous plaît.**
normal/super	**normale/super**
Check the oil/tires/battery, please.	**Veuillez contrôler l'huile/les pneus/la batterie.**
I've had a breakdown.	**Ma voiture est en panne.**
There's been an accident.	**Il y a eu un accident.**

E

ELECTRIC CURRENT. 220-volt, 50-cycle A.C. is now almost universal, though 110-volt may still be encountered in a few older parts of Tunis. Power surges are not unheard of, so it's best not to leave any appliance connected when not in use.

What's the voltage—110 or 220?	**Quel est le voltage—cent dix ou deux cent vingt?**
an adaptor plug/a battery	**une prise de raccordement/une pile**

112

EMERGENCIES. Depending on the nature of the problem, refer to the separate entries in this section such as CONSULATES, MEDICAL CARE, POLICE, etc.

Hotel staff are prepared to help in emergencies, as are local police and the Garde Nationale.

Emergency telephone numbers at Tunis:

Ambulance	261.200
Fire	198
Police	197

ENTRY FORMALITIES and CUSTOMS CONTROLS *(douane)*. Health certificates may be demanded from those coming from epidemic areas, but under normal circumstances they are not required. A valid passport is the only document necessary for nationals of the United States, Great Britain, Eire and Canada. United States citizens may stay four months, nationals of the other countries mentioned, three months. For nationals of Australia and New Zealand, visas are required with length of stay fixed at the time they are obtained.

Spot checks of tourists' luggage are carried out by Tunisian customs men, though in most cases a verbal declaration is sufficient to get you through quickly. The following chart shows what main duty-free items you may take into Tunisia and, when returning home, into your own country:

Into:	Cigarettes		Cigars		Tobacco	Spirits		Wine
Tunisia	200	or	50	or	400 g.	1 l.	or	1 l.
Australia	200	or	250 g.	or	250 g.	1 l.	or	1 l.
Canada	200	and	50	and	900 g.	1.1 l.	or	1.1 l.
Eire	200	or	50	or	250 g.	1 l.	and	2 l.
N. Zealand	200	or	50	or	½ lb.	1 qt.	and	1 qt.
U.K.	200	or	50	or	250 g.	1 l.	and	2 l.
U.S.A.	200	and	100	and	*	1 l.	or	1 l.

*no defined restrictions

E Besides personal effects, you are also allowed two cameras of different sizes or types, one cine-camera, and 20 rolls of film for each. Within reasonable limits, you can also bring in other items, and gifts up to a value of 10 Dinars.

Currency restrictions: The importation or exportation of Tunisian currency is prohibited. On the other hand, you can bring any amount of foreign currency into Tunisia, and take out up to the amount you imported. If you have Dinars left at the end of your stay, they can be converted for foreign currency by showing the *bordereau* (receipt) given you when you first changed your money. You will not be permitted to re-convert more than 30 per cent of the total amount of Dinars you bought during your stay, and in any case, you cannot re-convert more than 100 Dinars.

I've nothing to declare.	**Je n'ai rien à déclarer.**
It's for my personal use.	**C'est pour mon usage personnel.**

G **GUIDES and INTERPRETERS** *(guide; interprète)*. Tourist guides are licensed by the National Tourist Office and must carry an official identification badge and complaint book with them whenever on duty. The tourist office is the best place to contact a reputable guide who speaks English, as you can be sure you'll pay only the officially established rate for the region (see p. 103). Unofficial guides will approach you at every turn, but are not usually reliable.

Interpreters in many foreign languages may be hired in Tunis to help with business negotiations.

A.T.P.R. *(Agence Tunisienne de Public Relations)*, 6, Rue de Hollande, tel.: (01) 240.920.

V.I.P. AFRICA, Room 488, Hôtel Africa, Office Annex, tel.: (01) 242.423.

H **HAGGLING.** Many shops have fixed prices and the shopkeeper will tell you so (or post a sign saying *prix-fixe*), in which case bargaining will only annoy him. But in most shops in the *médina*, bargaining is acceptable. Small, inexpensive items are hardly worth haggling over, but large purchases demand discussion, perhaps a few glasses of mint tea, and a bit of friendly jousting before a price can be arrived at. If you take the trouble to get deeply into bargaining for an expensive carpet, you should do it in good will with the intention to buy if the final price is reasonable. On less expensive items, a few words (or astute moments

114

of silence) will usually result in a reduction of a Dinar or two. Unless the shop is a *prix-fixe* one, it always pays to haggle for at least a few moments, and it's expected. See also COMPLAINTS and page 90 in the Shopping section of this book.

HITCH-HIKING *(auto-stop)*. Because of slow and crowded inter-city bus service and lightly-trafficked highways, hitch-hikers are a common sight in Tunisia—most of them Tunisians. If you're hitch-hiking yourself, remember that patience is a virtue—it may be some while before you're picked up.

Can you give me a lift to…?	**Pouvez-vous m'emmener à …?**

HOTELS and ACCOMMODATION *(hôtel; logement)*. See also CAMPING and YOUTH HOSTELS. Tunisia's tourist industry has been established according to a master plan and facilities for accommodation haven't been left to chance. Resort hotels along Tunisia's coast are usually first-class, fairly well run and reasonably priced—especially if your room is included as part of a package tour. At times, single rooms can be somewhat expensive.

Tunis. Sousse. Gabès, Gafsa, Tozeur and Houmt Souk have a good range of hotels, and it's possible in these towns to find both bargain and luxury accommodation. All hotels are rated by the National Tourist Office *(Office National du Tourisme Tunisien*, or *O. N. T. T.)* and a sign displaying the hotel's "stars" is placed at the main entrance. On page 103, you'll find some typical minimum and maximum hotel rates for a double room with bath. The prices may or may not include a continental breakfast, depending on the hotel's policy. Rates should be quoted to you with service and taxes included, and prices must by law be posted in each room (usually on the back of the door).

Marhalas: The Touring Club of Tunisia and the Tunisian government have established a number of *marhalas* (simple inns) in various places more or less off the beaten track. In Houmt Souk, Kairouan and Nefta, the *marhalas* are set up in converted caravanserais; in Matmata there's one in a troglodyte dwelling; and in the far south several *ksars* (fortified villages) have been converted to offer simple, clean, inexpensive and very unusual accommodation to the traveller. Prices in the *marhalas* are only a Dinar or two per person, per night.

a single/double room	**une chambre à un lit/à deux lits**
What's the rate per night?	**Quel est le prix pour une nuit?**

L

LANGUAGE. See also ALPHABET. Tunisia is virtually a bilingual country and many Tunisians of Arabic or Berber stock speak French better than their "native" tongue. In the higher class hotels and restaurants, English is often spoken as well, but you cannot count on it being completely understood.

Even though French is widely spoken and written, some of the people in villages know no French. In fact, if it's a Berber village, they may not even know Arabic. But a few Arabic phrases will bring friendly smiles and assistance, providing you can approximate the rough, guttural sounds of Maghreb Arabic (accent equals stress).

Good morning	**S'báh 'l khéyr**
Good afternoon	**Msá 'l khéyr**
Good night	**Tis 'báh 'l khéyr**
Please	**Min fádlak**
Thank you	**Bárakallahúfik, shókran**
You're welcome	**Áfwen**
Goodbye	**Beslémeh**

LAUNDRY and DRY-CLEANING (*blanchissage; nettoyage à sec*). All hotels can arrange for laundry and dry-cleaning to be done. Laundry is often finished overnight, but dry-cleaning normally takes two or three days. In some cases faster service is available at a higher price. Dry-cleaning establishments and launderettes (*laverie self-service*) exist in most important towns and cities.

LOST PROPERTY. In cafés and restaurants, waiters and hotel staff will keep your forgotten hat, book or handbag safe at the *caisse* (cash desk); so the first thing to do when you discover you've lost something is to retrace your steps. If you left something on a bus or in a train or taxi, ask your hotel *concierge* to call and try to locate it. If all else fails, the Garde Nationale will help, or, in the cities, the police.

I've lost my wallet/handbag/ passport.	**J'ai perdu mon portefeuille/sac à main/passeport.**

LOUAGES. Called *voitures de louage*, or simply *louages* for short, these dusty station wagons, usually Peugeots, ply the main roads between Tunisian cities and towns. Faster and more dependable than inter-city buses, a trip by *louage* is quite inexpensive. Everybody uses this service, from government bureaucrats to maiden aunts.

In principle, a *louage* leaves when all seats are filled, which means you may have to wait a short while if you're the first to take a seat in the car. On the longer runs, however, it's often possible to reserve a seat in advance by telephoning a garage. Your hotel receptionist, or *concierge*, can help you make arrangements—and will direct you to the proper garage for departure.

MAPS. The English version of the O.N.T.T. (National Tourist Office) map can be recommended for its good, brief descriptions of Tunisia's sites and cities and adequately drawn road network. Main cities are also covered in a series of brochures issued by the National Tourist Office with titles such as *Map and Guide of Monastir.*

The maps in this book are by Falk-Verlag, Hamburg.

a street plan of...	**un plan de...**
a road map of this region	**une carte routière de cette région**

MEDICAL CARE. Make certain your health insurance will cover you while you're abroad and then relax and enjoy your holiday. If your home insurance cannot be extended to foreign countries, you may want to take out special travel insurance to pay for accident, illness and hospitalization for the duration of your trip.

Medical service is very well organized in Tunisia. Every city has at least one hospital and many large towns have hospitals or clinics staffed by the Public Health Service *(Service d'Hygiène)*. Telephone the Service d'Urgence (see next page) to visit a doctor at night (8 p.m.–7 a.m.) or on Sundays or holidays, or go to a hospital. Many foreign embassies and consulates keep lists of private clinics (mostly in Tunis) which they can recommend.

Chemists' or drugstores *(pharmacie)* are open during shopping hours. After hours, at least one pharmacy in each town stays open all night. The name and address of this *pharmacie de nuit* will be posted in the window of every other (closed) chemist's.

If you take medicine on a regular basis, it's best to bring a good supply, as Tunisian shops may not have the same brand you're used to.

The most common illnesses among tourists in Tunisia are caused by too much heat, either exterior from overexposure to the sun, or interior by eating too many plates of *mechouia* or other peppery and unfamiliar foods. Tunisian standards of hygiene are adequate and cause far less trouble to visitors than some visitors do to themselves.

M **Service de la Garde Médicale de la Ville de Tunis** *(Service d'Urgence)*, 32, Rue d'Allemagne; tel.: (01) 247.330 or 241.493.

I need a doctor/a dentist.	**Il me faut un médecin/dentiste.**
an ambulance/the hospital	**une ambulance/l'hôpital**
I have…	**J'ai…**
a sunburn/a sunstroke	**un coup de soleil/une insolation**
a fever/an upset stomach	**de la fièvre/une indigestion**

MEETING PEOPLE. Tunisians are hospitable and helpful in the traditional Arabic manner, which means that they may invite you home for tea, dinner or even to spend the night on the slightest pretext. Easy-going by nature, they are glad to be of help. They do not expect you to know Arabic and will greet you in French, whether they speak that language or not. If you should venture an Arabic greeting, the response will be enthusiastic (see LANGUAGE).

It's customary to shake hands at each encounter. The tradition-minded will then place his right hand (the one you shake with) briefly on his heart.

MONEY MATTERS

Currency: Tunisia's unit of currency is the *Dinar* (abbr. *D* or *TUD*), divided into 1,000 *Millimes* (abbr. *M*). Aluminium coins of 1, 2 and 5 Millimes may turn up in a handful of change, but most coins are copper (10, 20, 50 and 100 Millimes) or chromium steel ($^1/_2$ and 1 Dinar). There are bills of $^1/_2$, 1, 5, 10 and 20 (rare) Dinars. For currency restrictions see ENTRY FORMALITIES AND CUSTOMS CONTROLS.

Banking hours: Nothing about opening hours is sure, but between October 1st and July 1st, banks *(banque)* are *normally* open Monday–Friday from 8 to 11 a.m. and 2–4 p.m.; during the holy month of Ramadan from 8 to 11 a.m. and 1–2.30 p.m.; the rest of the year from 7.30 or 8 to 11 a.m. or 12 noon only. In major resorts a certain number of special branches are open to tourists during extended hours. In Tunis, the bank branches at some major hotels stay open seven days a week, holidays included, but with reduced hours in the low season. Airport exchange offices *(bureau de change)* work from 7 a.m. until the last flight arrives in the evening (if there's a lull, the clerk is liable to close the office and take a coffee break). Larger hotels and travel agencies are also authorized to change money, though the rate of exchange at these establishments will be less favourable. Be sure to keep the exchange receipts *(bordereau)* until you leave the country (see ENTRY FORMALITIES AND CUSTOMS CONTROLS).

Credit Cards and Traveller's Cheques: Major credit cards are accepted at the large hotels and at some restaurants, but you had better have cash if you venture into the *souks*. At the handicrafts shop of the Office National de l'Artisanat you'll get a 10 per cent discount for cash payment in a foreign currency as well as for traveller's cheques and credit cards.

Be sure to have your passport with you whenever you intend to use your credit card, exchange notes or pay with a traveller's cheque.

I would like to change some pounds/dollars.	**J'aimerais changer des livres sterling/des dollars.**
Do you accept traveller's cheques?	**Acceptez-vous les chèques de voyage?**
Can I pay with this credit card?	**Puis-je payer avec cette carte de crédit?**
Could you give me some (small) change?	**Pouvez-vous me donner de la (petite) monnaie?**

NEWSPAPERS and MAGAZINES *(journal; revue).* Hotel news-stands and kiosks in resort towns receive the most widely read British and Continental newspapers, including the *International Herald Tribune,* the day after publication. The selection is greatest at the height of the tourist season. Some British, Continental and American magazines are sold as well. There are several daily Tunisian newspapers in French as well as Arabic.

Have you any English-language newspapers/magazines?	**Avez-vous des journaux/revues en anglais?**

PHOTOGRAPHY. Most of the international brands of film are on sale in Tunisian camera shops, but more expensive than at home. Take full advantage of your duty-free film allowance (see ENTRY FORMALITIES AND CUSTOMS CONTROLS).

Local shops will process your black-and-white film in a day or two, but colour film may take a week or more. Under most circumstances it's easiest and best to have your film developed after you return home. Although there are numerous camera shops in the cities of Sousse and Tunis, they are not so easy to find in other areas.

P

Camera fees in Tunisian museums are high compared to entry fees and do not give you the right to use a tripod.

I'd like a film for this camera.	**Je voudrais un film pour cet appareil.**
a black-and-white film	**un film noir et blanc**
a film for colour prints	**un film couleurs**
a colour-slide film	**un film pour diapositives**
How long will it take to develop this film?	**Combien de temps faut-il pour développer ce film?**
Can I take a picture?	**Puis-je prendre une photo?**

POLICE *(police)*. Each Tunisian city has its own local police force to direct traffic, deal with complaints and apprehend lawbreakers. In Tunis, the force includes uniformed policewomen. Besides local forces, the Garde Nationale has stations in every city and town and patrols the highways. These forces work closely together and in practice it's hard to tell them apart as they all wear similar uniforms in grey, blue or brown. Collectively they are known in Arabic as *shorta*, from the French word *sûreté*. Virtually all police officers are bilingual in French and Arabic and make a particular point of being helpful to foreign visitors.

No country is ever free of pickpockets, but Tunisia is a relatively safe place. In crowded places, be sure to watch out for your camera, wallet or handbag. If you have anything of value which you cannot afford to lose, ask your hotel receptionist to put it in the safe.

Where's the nearest police station?	**Où est le poste de police le plus proche?**
I want to report a theft.	**Je veux signaler un vol.**
My ticket/wallet/passport has been stolen.	**On a volé mon billet/porte-feuille/passeport.**

PUBLIC HOLIDAYS *(jour férié)*. For practical purposes the Gregorian calendar is used widely in Tunisia. Nevertheless, the Moslem calendar, the *Hegira*, is followed by newspapers, employed in official documents and for certain movable public holidays and festivals (see p. 84).

The *Hegira* dates from the day of the emigration of the Prophet Mohammed from Mecca to Medina in 622 A.D. As the year is based on lunar months, there are only 354 days (or 355 in a leap year). This means that the *Hegira* year is 10 or 11 days shorter than the sidereal year and consequently the dates of the major religious festivals are always earlier than the year before. It also means that there's no relation between the months and the seasons.

The beginning of a new century in the *Hegira* calendar (1400 A.H.— *Anno Hegirae*) coincided with November 21st 1979. To calculate what year it is in the Moslem calendar subtract 579 from the Christian year.

On most public holidays museums remain open. During the month of Ramadan, banks, shops and business may have special opening hours, closing suddenly at dusk when the fast is broken as hungry workers head home for supper.

The dates listed below are the official non-religious public holidays of Tunisia:

January 1	*Jour de l'An*	New Year's Day
January 18	*Fête de la Révolution*	Revolution Day
March 20	*Fête de l'Indépen-dance*	Independence Day
April 9	*Anniversaire des Martyrs*	Martyrs' Day
May 1	*Fête du Travail*	Labour Day
June 1–2	*Fête nationale (Fête de la Victoire, Fête de la Jeunesse)*	Victory Day and Youth Day
July 25	*Fête de la République*	Republic Day
August 3	*Anniversaire du Pré-sident Bourguiba*	President Bourguiba's Birthday
August 13	*Fête de la Femme*	Woman's Day
September 3	*Anniversaire du Néo-Destour*	Memorial Day (1934)
October 15	*Fête de l'évacuation de Bizerte*	Evacuation Day (of Bizerta)

RADIO and TV *(radio; télévision).* Tunis has two radio stations broadcasting on the medium-wave band, one in Arabic and one in French. For a few hours each afternoon, the "French" station broadcasts in Italian. As Tunisia is so close to Europe, it's normally possible to pick up programmes in many European languages in the evening with just a simple transistor radio. The BBC World Service (after 10 p.m.) and the Voice of America (relayed from Crete) provide news and programmes in English.

R Tunisia's one television station broadcasts from 4 p.m. to midnight daily in Arabic, with a few hours of French-language programming after 9 or 10 p.m. Italian television is relayed from Sicily for viewers in northern Tunisia.

RELIGIOUS SERVICES. Tunisians are essentially Malikite Moslems, though there are a good number of Hanifite Moslems as well. Because of the French influence, Catholic churches exist in all cities and many large towns, including most resort towns. In Tunis, there are also French Protestant, Anglican and Greek Orthodox congregations.

Tunisia's Jewish community is an ancient one. There are two synagogues in Tunis and one on Djerba.

Hotels keep information on times of services and can direct you to your place of worship.

S **SIESTA.** Many shops, businesses and offices close between noon and 3 p.m., the hottest part of the day in summer. They re-open for several hours in the late afternoon and early evening.

T **TAXI.** See also LOUAGES. There are two types of taxi and it's important to know the difference. The large, highly-polished cars are known as *grands taxis* or *voitures de tourisme.* Sometimes they don't have meters. They are allowed to carry passengers anywhere in the country. The modest little cars with number signs on top are called *taxis-bébé* or just *taxis.* They all have meters and are allowed to carry up to three passengers only within city limits (and to airports; see p. 103). These mini-cabs are much cheaper than the larger ones (see p. 103). All taxis levy a 50 per cent surcharge for travel at night (10 p.m. to 6 a.m. April–September, 9 p.m. to 7 a.m. October–March) and can also charge extra for each piece of luggage. Tunisians generally don't tip taxi drivers, but rounding off the fare will always be appreciated.

What's the fare to…?   **Quel est le tarif pour…?**

TIME DIFFERENCES. Tunisian time is that of Western Europe—Central European Time (GMT + 1). Daylight saving time was tried once, in 1977, but not repeated.

Summer Time chart:

New York	London	**Tunisia**	Sydney	Auckland
7 a.m.	noon	**noon**	9 p.m.	11 p.m.

TIPPING. Tipping in Tunisia is not an absolute obligation—but it does mean more smiles and smoother service and is usually expected. Best in general round off bills and give the odd coin for services rendered.

Some suggestions:

Lavatory attendant	100 M
Maid/Manservant, per week	2–3 D
Porter, per bag	200 M
Taxi driver	round off
Tourist guide—official —"self-appointed"	5–7% of fee 100–200 M
Waiter	½–1 D or 5%

TOILETS *(toilettes).* Public toilets are rare except in large railway stations, airports and so on. By ordering a cup of coffee or a glass of wine in a café, you gain the right to use their facilities. Most hotels have toilets near the lobby and though they're meant for hotel guests and visitors, they'll hardly quibble if it's an emergency. In some toilets you may have to tip the attendant a few Millimes.

Where are the toilets, please? **Où sont les toilettes, s'il vous plaît?**

TOURIST INFORMATION OFFICES *(office du tourisme).* The Office National du Tourisme Tunisien (O.N.T.T.) maintains bureaus in all Tunisian cities and resort areas and in many cities abroad. The head office is in Tunis at

1, Avenue Mohamed V; tel.: (1) 259 133, telex 12381.

Canada: Représentation de l'Office Tunisien du Tourisme, 18, Frontenac, Case Postale 1233, Place Bonaventure, Montréal, Québec H5A lGl; tel.: (514) 866-1621.

Great Britain: Tunisian Tourist Office, 7a, Stafford Street, London W1; tel.: (01) 930-1103.

T **U.S.A.:** Tunisian Tourist Office, 630 Fifth Avenue, Suite 863, New York, N.Y. 10020; tel.: (212) 582-3670.

Tourist offices within Tunisia are open during normal business hours.

Where's the tourist office, please? **Où est le Syndicat d'Initiative, s'il vous plaît?**

TRAINS *(train)*. The Société Nationale des Chemins de Fer Tunisiens *(S. N. C. F. T.)* operates several lines of interest to tourists. The narrow-gauge track from Tunis to Hammamet and Nabeul is very convenient, taking only about $1\frac{1}{2}$ hours to Hammamet. Tunis to Bizerta takes about 2 hours. For longer trips south—from Tunis to Sousse (3 hours), El Djem (4 hours) and Gabès (7 hours)—it's best to pay the supplement for a seat in the *voiture grand confort* (luxury-class car). Tickets are not expensive. Timetables are hard to find and you may have to go to the station to find out current departure times.

The *Transmaghreb Express* will take you the 1,000 kilometres from Tunis to Algiers in less than 20 hours; sleeping cars are available.

The *T.G.M. (Tunis–Goulette–Marsa)* electric train is the best way to get from Tunis to Carthage, Sidi Bou Saïd, and La Marsa. Trains leave every 12 minutes from the foot of Avenue Habib Bourguiba. Children between four and ten travel half fare.

W **WATER** *(eau)*. Most tap water in Tunisia is quite safe to drink and is served at table in cafés. But with meals, Tunisians prefer bottled mineral water, either still or fizzy, which takes the place of wine or beer which, as good Moslems, they are not supposed to drink. You needn't be worried about the water except in out-of-the-way villages.

Y **YOUTH HOSTELS.** Called either *auberge de jeunesse* or *maison de jeunes,* youth hostels (in fact, there's no age limit) are located in all major towns and resorts. Rules are similar to those in force at hostels in Europe and you should have a membership card from your national youth hostel organization, although they may let you in without a card if there are empty places. (For average rates, see p. 103.) A list of hostels and hints on how to reach them by public transport can be obtained from the Association Tunisienne des Auberges de Jeunesse:

124 63, Avenue Habib Bourguiba (2nd floor), Tunis; tel.: (01) 246.000.

DAYS OF THE WEEK

Sunday	**dimanche**	Thursday	**jeudi**
Monday	**lundi**	Friday	**vendredi**
Tuesday	**mardi**	Saturday	**samedi**
Wednesday	**mercredi**		

MONTHS

January	**janvier**	July	**juillet**
February	**février**	August	**août**
March	**mars**	September	**septembre**
April	**avril**	October	**octobre**
May	**mai**	November	**novembre**
June	**juin**	December	**décembre**

NUMBERS

0	**zéro**	19	**dix-neuf**
1	**un, une**	20	**vingt**
2	**deux**	21	**vingt et un**
3	**trois**	22	**vingt-deux**
4	**quatre**	23	**vingt-trois**
5	**cinq**	30	**trente**
6	**six**	40	**quarante**
7	**sept**	50	**cinquante**
8	**huit**	60	**soixante**
9	**neuf**	70	**soixante-dix**
10	**dix**	71	**soixante et onze**
11	**onze**	80	**quatre-vingts**
12	**douze**	90	**quatre-vingt-dix**
13	**treize**	100	**cent**
14	**quatorze**	101	**cent un**
15	**quinze**	126	**cent vingt-six**
16	**seize**	200	**deux cents**
17	**dix-sept**	300	**trois cents**
18	**dix-huit**	1000	**mille**

SOME USEFUL EXPRESSIONS

yes/no	oui/non
please/thank you	s'il vous plaît/merci
excuse me	excusez-moi
you're welcome	je vous en prie
where/when/how	où/quand/comment
how long/how far	combien de temps/à quelle distance
yesterday/today/tomorrow	hier/aujourd'hui/demain
day/week/month/year	jour/semaine/mois/année
left/right	gauche/droite
up/down	en haut/en bas
good/bad	bon/mauvais
big/small	grand/petit
cheap/expensive	bon marché/cher
old/new	vieux/neuf
open/closed	ouvert/fermé
here/there	ici/là
free (vacant)/occupied	libre/occupé
early/late	tôt/tard
easy/difficult	facile/difficile
Does anyone here speak English?	Y a-t-il quelqu'un ici qui parle anglais?
What does this mean?	Que signifie ceci?
I don't understand.	Je ne comprends pas.
Please write it down.	Ecrivez-le-moi, s'il vous plaît.
Is there an admission charge?	Faut-il payer pour entrer?
Waiter/Waitress!	Garçon/Mademoiselle!
I'd like…	J'aimerais…
How much is that?	C'est combien?
Have you something less expensive?	Avez-vous quelque chose de moins cher?
What time is it?	Quelle heure est-il?
Help me please.	Aidez-moi, s'il vous plaît.
Get a doctor—quickly!	Un médecin, vite!

126

Index

An asterisk (*) next to a page number indicates a map reference.

Aïn Draham   39*, 77
Aïn Oktor   39*, 42

Bardo, see Museums
Beaches   51, 58, 76, 77
Bizerta   39*, 75, 76
Bourguiba, Habib   21, 22, 46
Bulla Regia   39*, 77

Cap Bon   38–42, 39*
Cap Negro   39*, 77
Cap Serrat   39*, 77
Cap Tourgueness   51–52, 61*
Carpets   49, 87–88
Carthage   10, 11, 13, 31–34, 39*
Chebika   61*, 73
Chenini   61*, 62–63
Chott (salt lake)
   el Djérid   60, 61*, 68
   el Fedjedj   61*, 68

Djébel Tebaga (mountains)
   61*, 68
Djemnah (Jemnah)   61*, 68–69
Djerba, Ile de   51–58, 61*
Dougga   37, 39*
Douiret   61*, 63
Douz   61*, 69

El Djem   39*, 49–50
El Hamma   61*, 68
El Haouaria   39*, 42
Eriadh   57

Festivals   42, 69, 84–85, 120–121
Folklore   54, 82–84
Food   92–95, 98–99, 103
Foum Tataouine   61*, 62

Gabès   61*, 66
Gafsa   61*, 70
Ghar el Melh   39*, 76
Ghorfas (granaries)   60, 62, 63
Ghoumrassen   61*, 65
Guellala   57–58, 61*
Guermessa   61*, 63

Hammamet   38–40, 39*
Hannibal   13
Houmt Souk   55–57, 61*

Kairouan   39*, 46–49
Kasbas (forts)   40, 44, 76
Kébili   61*, 68
Kélibia   39*, 42
Kerkouane   39*, 42
Korbous   39*, 42
Ksar Haddada   61*, 65
Ksars (fortified villages)   62, 63

La Galite, Ile de   39*, 77
La Ghriba   57, 61*
Language   22, 38, 40, 105, 116

Mahboubine   58, 61*
Marhalas (inns)   65, 115
Markets (see also Shopping and
   Souks)   57, 58, 69
Matmata   61*, 66, 68

Médenine   61*, 62

Médinas
  Hammamet   40
  Sousse   43–44
  Tunis   25*, 26–31
Métameur   61*, 62
Midès   61*, 75
Midoun   58, 61*
Monastir   39*, 45–46
Mosques   73
  Bourguiba (Monastir)   46
  Djamâ ez Zitouna (Tunis)
    25*, 26–27
  Djamâ Tleta Bibane
    (Kairouan)   48
  Grand Mosque (Bizerta)   76
  Grand Mosque (Kairouan)
    48
  Grand Mosque (Monastir)   46
  Grand Mosque (Sousse)   43
  Hammoûda Pacha (Tunis)
    25*, 31
  Sidi Sahab (Kairouan)   48
Museums   44, 50, 52, 77, 85
  Bardo (National Museum,
    Tunis)   37
  Dar ben Abdallah (Museum of
    Folklore and Popular Arts,
    Tunis)   25*, 31
  Dar Hussein (Museum of
    Islamic Art, Tunis)   25*, 28,
    30–31
  Ibrahim ibn el Aghlab
    (Museum of Islamic Art,
    Kairouan)   48
  Museum of Folklore and
    Popular Arts, Gabès)   66
  Museum of Folklore and
    Popular Arts (Houmt
    Souk)   55–56
  National Museum of
    Carthage   32–33

Nabeul   39*, 40–42
Nefta   61*, 73
Nightlife   90–91

Oases   58, 65–75

Pottery   40–41, 42, 57–58

Raf-Raf   39*, 76
Restaurants, see Food
Romans   11, 13, 33, 34, 37, 44,
  49, 50, 70, 75, 77

Safaris   80
Sahel   39*, 42–46
Sbeïtla (Sufetula)   37, 39*
Sedjenane   39*, 77
Sfax   39*, 50, 61*
Shopping (see also Markets and
  Souks)   42, 86–90
Sidi Ali el Mekki   39*, 76
Sidi Bou Saïd   34–37, 39*
Sidi Daoud   39*, 42
Sidi Mechrig   39*, 77
Souks   28, 44, 49, 56–57
Sousse   39*, 43–44
Sports   51, 77, 79–82

Tabarka   39*, 77
Tamerza   61*, 75
Thuburbo Majus   37, 39*
Tozeur   61*, 70–73
Tunis   24–31, 25*, 39*
Turks   18–20, 31, 49–50, 56, 76

Utica   10, 39*, 77

Wine   42, 95

Zarzis   58, 61*
Zembra, Ile de   39*, 42